Contents

INTRODUCTION: 7
MAY 2023 9
THIS ISN'T A BOOK... 12
WHERE'S WALLY-NICO? 13
    Morphine 14
WHY AM I IN A MENTAL HOSPITAL? 15
STOP THE CRAZY TRAIN FOR A MINUTE 24
WHAT IS IT LIKE IN HERE? 27
    The Drive Here: 27
        First Admission: 27
        Second Admission: 28
    Booking Into Hospital: 30
    Suicide Watch 32
    Toilet And Shower Facilities 33
    Shovelling Food 34
        Typical Mealtimes; 35
    Activities 36
        Pottery 38
    Bedrooms 41
MEN VS WOMEN 42
        Interlude 43
CHAIRNESS 44
ESCAPE IS A GLASS PANE AWAY 46
DICK ON A DONKEY 48

- Dick on a Donkey 52
- DETECTIVE MILLER 55
- THE SHITTY FORK IN THE ROAD 58
- JOB INTERVIEWS 62
- THE ROAD TO RECOVERY 63
  - Fun Interlude 64
- DAY-WHATEVER 66
  - My mind is La Brea 67
- HEALTH UPDATE WHATEVER 68
- THE PEACH PIT 69
  - They've already lost 70
- CORONATION DAY 71
- CORONATION DAY – Take 2 74
  - Fun Interlude 76
- DREAMS 78
  - Cat Nightmare 79
  - Some worst nightmares 80
    - Rescuing people from Nazis; 80
    - Nazi Nightmare 2 83
- LAUNDRY 85
  - The Thin Glass Pane 87
  - Farewell My Friend 89
- UNEXPECTED VISIT 91
- NEXT STEPS 92
  - Fun Interlude 93
- MONDAY 1 MAY 2023 ... OH – "MY MONTH" 94
- A GOOD DAY 97

"Fun" – rather tragic really – Interlude 98
MONDAY 15 May 101
    Parsimonious 102
NEW KEYBOARD!! 103
    Sleeping lions 104
ON: THE SPEED OF LIGHT 105
THE PODCAST 106
HACKSAW RIDGE 108
THE JOB INTERVIEW 111
    Death's Hour 112
CHRISTOPHE'S GIFT 113
    The Anvil Has Been Struck 115
THE ANOREXIA TABLE 117
A SMALL MEASURE OF PEACE 123
    The Mortal wound 125
SATURDAY VISIT 127
ANGELS IN BLUE AND GREEN 128
SURPRISE EUTHANASIA 130
THE YELLOW FLOWER 136
    Meadow Buttercup 138
THE BLUE TOYOTA HILUX 139
    Scheduled Maintenance 144
THE JOB INTERVIEW 146
FINAL HOURS 149
    FINAL WEEK 151
THE JOB IS A NO 152
    Peace to you 152

THIS IS AWKWARD…	153
THE HORNET IN THE BOURBON	153
FRIDAY 9 JUNE 2023 – Last quick update	154
The Hurricane	156
SATURDAY 17 JUNE	159
SYNAESTHESIA…	162
CHANGE OF TACK…	164
FALL OF THE TITAN	168
ODE TO A TITAN	170
IT'S ALIVE!	172
MENTAL HEALTH DISCRIMINATION	175
FUNNY STORY ABOUT AN ACQUAINTANCE	177
Hypocrisy	178
FRIENDSHIPS	179
EMPATHS	182
GREY CLOUDS	186
Precipice	188
The Hurricane	190
BIRTHDAY	192
The river of Time	193
ACTUAL BIRTH DATE AND DAY	194
IT'S SO EASY	196
POST BIRTHDAY BLUES	198
SUICIDE IS NOT THAT EASY	201
IN THE FINAL ANALYSIS	203
TOMORROW IS A GOOD DAY TO DIE	206
THE DAY AFTER I DIE	209

- THE DAY AFTER I DIED 210
  - The Dream; 213
    - Journey's End 217
- SINÉAD O'CONNOR 218
- HELLO OLD FRIEND! 220
  - Life's Storms 223
- STILL LOOKING FOR WORK 224
- PIPPIN! Well, just PIP 226
- I WILL TAKE THE RING TO MORDOR… 228
- OK, LET'S LAND THIS PLANE… 230
  - "What did I learn this year?" 231
    - What did you learn about others? 231
    - What did you learn about yourself that wasn't there 232
    - How did you come to grips with not working? How have you found the strength to get up in the morning? 233
- TEMET NOSCE – "KNOW THYSELF" 235
  - ADHD – a bigger deal than people know 235
  - Synaesthesia: 238
- WHY IS AN ADHD AND AUTISM DIAGNOSIS IMPORTANT? 242
  - AUTISM 243
  - ADHD 244
- LANDING GEAR DOWN, FULL FLAPS 245
- POTENTIAL NEW RESEARCH FOR MENTAL HEALTH (Mental Health people, please read) 249
- THE CHEQUERED FLAG – FINALLY 254

INTRODUCTION:

20 May 2024
1 Year after starting this; Spoiler, I survived 2023.

The writing in this "book" is something that should probably never see the light of day. At least it did not start off with the idea of being a book. I was bored to tears in the mental hospital, and writing was cathartic.

TRIGGER WARNING; BEYOND THIS POINT THERE ARE MANY REFERENCES TO SUICIDE, SELF-HARM AND DEATH. PLEASE DO NOT READ IF THAT UPSETS YOU.

This was certainly never written to be a book or for people to read. Like I say somewhere, it was meant to be a mirror for my own reflection later – if I ever got better.

But over the year I've had some "robust" conversations with many people and many of them have expressed their thoughts – their desire – to read something like this. Certainly, Mental Health professionals suggested they'd like to read it.

I've also seen many people saying they would like to read something like this to understand maybe some of the thoughts their loved ones went through before they ended their own lives.

Please know that none of this is meant to be a diagnostic tool for other people. This was just me reflecting on my own turmoil and my eventual emergence from it. But, if even one person is able to find any kind of comfort or solace from this, it would have been worth it.

The writing here for the most part is unfiltered, raw and pretty damn painful. I struggled to read some of this a year on, it's horrific. I cannot imagine what it would be for someone not in a crisis and who has not experienced what I did.

I BEG FOR CLEMENCY THOUGH. I think the fact that I am horrified by what I wrote shows I am not the same as what I was then. Please do not judge me for what I wrote here – it was a terrible, dark time!

But I decided to publish this in the vain hope that if my awful year and what I wrote in here helps just one other human, it would have been worth everything! Not everything is necessarily in perfect chronological order (much of it is).

There are a lot of issues – from grammar, formatting (I tried to tidy it), structure, flow etc. Take that as a sign that this was definitely not written to publish ever. I certainly did not expect this to exceed 63,000 words!

But it's written and universally pretty much every health and mental health professional I've spoken to have said they'd love to read something like this to understand how suicidal thoughts flow in people's minds.

There's also a lot of "poetry" in here. I hate poetry. I hate poems. Like the worst form of literature on earth. But it's here. Why? Dunno. Take it as a sign that I am not an author and not particularly skilled in the use of language

Also, this does not really apply to specific individuals – aside from a few specific references. If you read anything and take offence – that's your choice. This was written by me when I was actively *planning* suicide. I rambled in the dark and argued with myself and the world at large. If you do take offence, maybe sit and think of the weight and burden of darkness that was on me and to have gone through every agonising minute.

Finally, I mention the imminent nature of dying often. This can maybe be a pointer to mental health professionals and loved ones of people who do go through with suicide – that it's rarely a random thought that pops into your head on a Tuesday morning. It's a tumultuous, fierce squall of a storm that rages internally between your most basic will to survive and your equally most primal will to end pain.

MAY 2023

This "Not a Book" contains some very sensitive topics – well, topics which normal, healthy (mentally healthy!) people might find sensitive. Seriously, PLEASE DO NOT READ IF THE MENTION OF SUICIDE, SELF-HARM OR DEATH UPSETS YOU.

I am broken.

Broken upon broken.

Imagine taking a glass pane and hitting it with a hammer. Then take the bits of glass shards and bash them repeatedly until just a bit of glass dust is left over. That is pretty much how broken my spirit is. It's not a subtle bit of broken or cracks. My spirit is crushed into glass dust. Just getting a bit of glue won't fix it. Sadly, I don't know how to fix it, as a large part of my brokenness is because of my broken body which cannot be fixed (or so I've been told).

This piece of writing is full of self-doubt, self-insults, swear words enough to make a pirate baulk. It's about what may – or may not – turn out to be my final month, days and hours on this planet.

Consider these words of this "Not a Book" the ramblings of a dying man, so deep in agony on so many levels, that he actively seeks death. It contains ironic and tragic humour at places. I mostly wrote it as a mirror to reflect on if I were to survive May 2023. But I am feeling less and less likely to survive, certainly no way beyond July.

There are many, MANY parts of this "Not a Book" that I shouldn't have written. Things that on balance nobody should ever write – that I should definitely not have written. But I didn't delete them, in order to remain true to my struggle and authentic.

These are MY experiences as I try to meander this mental health mess that I am in. Please do not form any basis or opinion on anyone or anything based on my inane rambling.

I did not write this with the eye on it ever seeing the light of day. This started off as a digital diary of sorts to help me recall the last few months. But as I've met other people and read online, it occurred to me that there are MANY self-help books on Mental health, and many Mental-health related topics – most if not all which focus on how to get better.

Few that I've seen actually document the descent through the chaos. And so I thought that perhaps, if I survived, someone might find this of use to either understand the darkness a suicidally depressed mind goes through, the struggles and issues they face (or at least I face), and maybe be able to support their loved ones better.

Because I will tell you that my teetering on the edge of suicide has not felt like cowardice or running away from my problems. It has, and continues to be, a very real, very difficult struggle to survive. To justify why I deserve to live.

By the way, there are 96 bags of poop on the Moon.

I tried anonymise this, as I do not want anyone pointing to an absolutely incredible staff in the mental hospital, nor do I want to bring shame or judgement to the patients. This is just my own idiocy and carelessness that caused all this shit, and ultimately the only moron responsible.

So read this with the caution that it isn't going to be the lightest reading you've ever seen, and that I am a monster. Read on at your own peril...

A quick example of how inappropriate I can be; At a work Christmas party once, I thought I'd "push the boat out" and engage socially. Glass of Coca Cola in my hand, I stood with a group of colleagues who were talking about holiday – one was going on holiday to Cape Town in South Africa. Being intimately familiar with CT, I asked what they had planned. They mentioned shark cage diving, which was my perfect segway to a funny story. I explained with great laughter about a video I saw of one of those semi-rigid inflatable boats around Cape Town, where a shark swam right up to the boat and bit it, deflating it. I even showed the video. It was hilarious! Only, it was apparently not.

My manager later said to me *"Mon dieu Nico! I asked you to be more you and engage socially more, but not like this! That is not even a funny story, those poor people."* Horrified at my apparent social faux pas, I explained that the shark didn't actually eat the people, they got away safely. But that was apparently not the point. I had failed to read social cues and told a horrifying story in a completely incorrect way. Who was to know? I certainly have no idea when something is appropriate or not. Blame my Autism and ADHD brain for that.

By the way, the video is still online. Look for it on YouTube for a laugh. You'll see it is pretty funny.

Point is, I do not "get" the social thing, and I do not always understand what it appropriate or inappropriate. I'd gladly jump right into a new conversation with someone I've just met and talk about my views on Suicide for example. But apparently this is not appropriate.

Maybe that is why the mental health team locked me up, the fact that I was not able to think of what might be inappropriate and therefore did not filter what I said….

THIS ISN'T A BOOK... (It's a "Not a Book")

A friend from church came to visit yesterday (11 May 2023)... WHY DO I EVEN PUT THE STUPID DATES IN??? I am an odd idiot. Actually – might be some reason for my insanity, maybe the dates will make this jumble of mess easier to organise? Not that anyone but myself will ever read this cluster-fuck. Thankfully!

Anyway, I was talking to her about something I had written in this – whatever this is. I referred to it as a "book", then quickly corrected myself and said *"Well, it's not a book, it's just a collection of pages"*.

Not sure if she was mentally aligned when the sudden, utterly bizarre notion dawned on me that *all books are a collection of pages.* Whether or not the word "just" is justified is up for debate. The Gutenberg Bible for example is so much more than *just* a few pages. A very vehemently atheistic friend of mine once shocked me by saying that he thought the Gutenberg Bible is one of the most important works ever created by Man, as it represented the dawn of the *"Age of Reason"*. Pretty sure that quote is from the movie "Day After Tomorrow" – a firm favourite of mine.

Of course, the Gutenberg Bible is so much more than just the aesthetic and historical value. In a time when the Roman Catholic Church held sway, had monopoly over God if you will, the Gutenberg Bible was really more than a book and rather the start of an Information Age.

But *this*, this thing you are reading – well, for now it's just some pages with some words from the alphabet. It's "Not a Book". Who knows – maybe if I were someone famous, this could have been something. But I am just some apparently deluded, fat guy in Wales in a mental hospital. Compared to the Gutenberg Bible, my name and work will be like a fart in the wind. Unimportant, and unnoticed

So take whatever I say with an industrial digger of salt...

WHERE'S WALLY-NICO?

Every word I type is from "my" yellow chair in the common room in the mental health ward in a Mental Hospital in Wales – an acute Mental Health Admission Ward. OK, that is not entirely factually correct – I've typed a few words from the blue chair. But the blue chairs are either too far from the window, or they have your back to patients. I don't like sitting with my back to people, because you cannot see if someone is coming to stab you...

I am not here because I *wanted* to be here.
I am not here because I asked or cried for help.
I am not here because I wanted help.

Let's just be perfectly clear about that.

On a Sunday at the end of August 2018, I injured my back whilst carrying a wooden beehive frame called a super, which was full to the brim of glorious honey. My foot slipped in mud, and whilst in a very clumsy bee suit, carrying this precious load of honey, my efforts weren't on my back, but rather to not harm the bees, and save the honey.

I might address the back injury in more detail if I end up writing more. Suffice to say that I hurt my back badly in the fall. Already weakened from slipping down stairs in 2011, one of the discs between the vertebrae in my lower spine ruptured. This caused the vertebrae to grind on each other. I went to work the next day, barely able to dress myself or even put shoes on, I caught a lift with a colleague. But slowly, the Monday turned into a living hell of pain so severe I could not breathe.

Initially, the 1,200 tablets, and the first 500ml bottle of Morphine I was given *every month* was funny – amusing rather. The second one a month later was slightly less amusing. Nearly 5 years, I've had ~70,000 tablets and in excess of 29 *litres* of Morphine. I've even lost 2-3cm of height, as the discs in my back are so damaged

MORPHINE

The bottles of morphine are no longer amusing.
Each bottle part of a link in a chain that holds me captive.
Like a hook in the mouth of a fish.
Something you didn't want
but dug its claws into your very soul.

Each link of Morphine now
a reaffirmation of a pain that will never end

Of a spine that will never mend.
Of dignity that will never be restored.
Of freedom that will never be regained.
Of a life that has become an existence.
Of a soul no longer dreaming of the future,
but instead yearning for the end.

The end of the pain
or the end of the existence
it doesn't really matter anymore
It is clear that these are inextricably linked

WHY AM I IN A MENTAL HOSPITAL?

Beats me. I. AM. NOT. DEPRESSED.

Trying to not swear too much - but either put your big boy pants on or put the book down if you don't like the occasional, strategically-placed F-word from a broken man in a mental health hospital ☺

I am here because 4 Psychiatrists and Psychologists in one room, over the course of a number of sessions, decided that I am mentally ill and officially Sectioned me under the Mental Health act of 1983. I was ... *"sassy"* ... with them when they initially announced the *punishment* of Sectioning me. It really did feel like a court execution order.

I asked all four of them what kind of tech or equipment they still use from 1983. That was not so well received. The one doctor pointed out that the Mental Health act was revised in 2002. I repeated the question, as the fact stood for itself. That also, was not well received. I mean who uses anything from 2002?

Thinking back, and reading the notes that I managed to see from the people in charge, I also assaulted their ethics, which didn't please them much. I'll get into the ethics later...

Unbeknownst to me, long before my jail sentence was passed, they had ordered a special "Jail-bulance" from Birmingham – with 1 driver and 3 pretty big burly guys and one lady to conduct me to this facility. Side-note, I sized up all 3 guys in the very well caged up Jail-bulance and I reckon I could probably not have handled all 3 of them. But at least dished out some injury in a failed escape attempt. My back might be messed up, but I grew up under the harsh African sun and have a body which reflects that. That's all I will say on that. The lady in the Jail-bulance, I assumed was there as an attempted calming influence to speak to my lost humanity if I decided to act out.

OK, I am not in a jail – it is (if I am honest) a fairly nice and comfortable facility that feels less like an actual hospital and more like a hostel or something where you stay with a bunch of strangers.

ANYWAY...

I am here because I am so fed up of pain and agony, night and day.

Lying awake night after night, sleeping 3, maybe 5 hours on a *good* night. I feel like I am trapped in a broken meat cage where every moment is filled with agony. It's like a canvas painted in blood, and despite a pretty picture painted over it, the blood and pain remain.

Philosophically, I deeply disagree with my detention.

Ethically, I disagree quite profoundly with my detention.

Not even sure what victory they think they won, or purpose they achieved, other than prolonging my suffering and torture... oh and draining valuable NHS resources even more. I mean if they think they won a victory, boy, do they have a surprise coming! People so often go on about how smart they are – and honestly if you need to tell people you're smart, you probably suffer from the Dunning-Kruger effect. But I will say that *in this instance*, <u>I've been severely underestimated, *dear Doctor*</u> ;)

As the psychologists "sentenced" me, I was sipping from an energy drink can. Realising they were not going to be convinced about not locking me up, I picked the metal pull-tab off the can. In my manic mindset, I thought I could maybe sharpen the pull-tab to become a cutting instrument to use on myself.

But back to why I not only philosophically, and also ethically disagree with my *detention*;

I have lost my honour, my dignity and my worth to society.

I've become little more than a bad smell that lingers in a room. I have no more value to anyone – I'm like a virus that consumes and provides little else of worth.

My honour is lost.
That's the worst.

In ancient Japan, the Bushido code demanded a fallen, dishonoured warrior take their own life in order to restore their honour. If I'd had a Second, I'd have gladly committed Seppuku, I have an exquisite folded-steel Tanto just for that purpose. Wonder if they'd let me bring it to hospital...? A Second in this context means a warrior to decapitate you, once you've stabbed and cut your stomach.

But since I didn't have a Second, I had to research other ways of ending a life that is well past sell-by date Which is when the assholes tracked my internet searches and alerted the police. Lesson here I guess, is to invest in a proper VPN.

Funny story;
When I first went to speak to the GP about why I feel suicidal, he was distressed and bemused in equal measure that I was more upset at being caught out than anything else! He laughed actually. Couldn't believe the absurdity that I was "more pissed off at being caught, than anything else". Don't get why he was so bemused.

But then, I have autism.

I rarely get humour. I often just stare at people when they tell jokes, waiting for the punchline to be explained.

Anyway, so my *incarceration*...

The GP and Crisis Team wanted me to go in "for a chat".

Me being ever the naive, considerate and caring twat who feels deeply for others; I didn't want anyone of my primary carers to be implicated in my imminent suicide, which is why I quietly tried to research it. When I was caught out, I merely went along with all the sessions in order for the doctors of whatever speciality, to be able to honestly tell the Coroner that they did all they could. So that they could remain innocent and not even feel an ounce of personal guilt. Not in my wildest ~~dreams~~ nightmares did I think I'd end up being sectioned.

Which is cruel. This is cruel.

During every session, I believed that I was able to very clearly, calmly and with unassailable logic explain how I ended at the decision to end my life. Why it was only right. Good and proper that I die. Why I am a waste of oxygen and more useless than an underwater chocolate hairdryer.

It was my understanding that they were making notes to provide to the Coroner when they collect the corpse. Not to catch me out and punish me by locking me up here.

Objectively, every part of my life has now been made worse. I'm unemployed as I write this – have been since end January (still by November 2023). Money is getting tighter and without being able to financially contribute to my family, I am worth less than nothing – especially as I cannot do DIY and other helpful things due to my "*sore wuttle back*".
Useless cunt.
Pathetic pussy that cannot handle a boo-boo.

So in the spirit of Bushido – I, *as a man robbed* of dignity, honour and value, decided to end my life.

But I was stopped.

I was stopped, and subsequently *punished* for my unforgivable sin of not thinking like the psychiatrist team. For not sharing in their beliefs of what a human life is worth. Life is not all that precious dumbass.

I was also punished for telling the truth.

Punished for being completely open and sincere, measured in every word. Seems perverse almost. They have a certain set of values, which I am being subject to, despite me having my very own values which have served me well enough for 44 years! That'll teach me to tell the truth. Next time just lie and say I am fine?

Can you believe though, that they said in their official notes, that *I AM DELUDED*, and under the delusional belief that I don't have a mental disorder. De-fucking-luded!? Not a word of a lie. They called me deluded for stating that I do not have a mental disorder. I've had bloody enough of a life filled with pain, Morphine and other stuff hooked in my mouth like a fish. That's what I have. *Fed-up-from-painness* yes.

But a mental disorder? I think not. I mean to me personally, this ... "collection of words and pages" is pretty clearly, and rationally thought out and written. Not sure if many/any of the fellow patients with me are even able to articulate half of what I've written. So many of them seem so "out of it" aside from maybe one or two. They are like NPCs in computer games (Non-Player Characters – robots, a thing the computer made that looks human, but is just a robot)

OH!

Don't even get me started on the vaunted morality of the "value of life"! The "value of life" is probably one of the biggest hypocrisies in the world.

If we discovered even the simplest of living microbes on another planet, much of the world would collapse in anarchy. Entire religious systems would collapse if even the simplest life were discovered on another planet. Social chaos would likely ensue, as people's entire belief systems came crashing down. We'd spend billions researching it. We'd invent new types of spaceship to go to the planet to study the microbes. Scientists' entire careers would be made and revolve around studying the alien microbes.

And yet, every day there are untold numbers of abortions committed on Earth (I don't even want to Google the number tbh).

Growing foetuses – unborn children in the safest place they could be – are summarily executed and disposed of with barely an inconvenience. So what makes my broken, pain-filled life worth any bit more than an unborn child? And murders – so many murders daily, and that's not even counting wars where one wanker is in a dick measuring contest with another wanker and sends young people to die.

Humans and their bloody hypocrisy!!

I disagree most strongly that other people's will is forced on me.

Years ago, when this back pain started getting too much, when I first thought of going to Dignitas in Switzerland, the NHS refused to help.

When I still saw a future, when I still had hope for myself, I *begged* the NHS to help.

Help, being an artificial disc replacement. It would have helped, I am sure. And whilst there is risk, it couldn't be worse than where I've ended up now, is there? I mean I have actively been trying to kill myself – how is that worse than whatever risk they imagined?

There are fates worse than death you know? *I certainly know*!

And yet, with a twisted sense of humour, I was given 1,200 pills and a half litre of morphine every month. Told to fuck off and stop bothering them for another month – go get wasted on your own damn Morphine...

Repeatedly the NHS said no to the operation.

Then, when I nearly died from the *in excess of 200mg Morphine per day*, they injected me with an evil drug called Naloxone – boy was that an event. The videos my wife took of that event still chill me to the bone.

So the Morphine was taken away and replaced with something less useful. My fault apparently, for being in constant pain and nearly dying from morphine which had been prescribed and I took carefully and to the letter.

Enter the amazing Doctor ... I'll call her "Lisa", in order to protect her anonymity. What a godsend that woman was. She did more – arguably more than all doctors and specialists combined between December 2021 and April 2023. She referred me to a spinal hospital for hydrotherapy. She walked a long, hard road with me to review meds often and help get me fixed. Which she did. I was – I am so profoundly grateful to her.

Unfortunately – either she herself, or the Practice – withdrew her from my case after she heard about my suicidal thoughts and me explaining my reasons with the rationality and clarity of mind you'd expect of a dispassionate third party. Not heard from her since.

In September 2022, on the referral of the amazing Doctor Lisa, I attended the absolutely amazing Robert Jones, Agnes Hunt Orthopaedic hospital in Gabowen. What a bloody amazing group of people there. I arrived needing to lean heavily on my walking stick. After 2 weeks, I was able to walk out mostly unassisted.

I made changes to my diet (chiefly cutting out full-sugar Coca Cola), and started walking "recreationally". I bought into an app called Conqueror, which tracked my steps as I walk, and overlaid it with the Lord of the Rings journey from the Shire to Mordor. I made it my mission to carry my "One Ring" – my back pain – to Mordor and rid myself of it. As in, walk and walk, lose weight, get fit and build strength. And damn man, I put the effort in. More on good days, less on worse days.

Between 1 October 2022 and 29 April 2023, I walked a little under 200 miles. This, for someone whom walking just to get to the toilet is sometimes a 10 minute journey – frankly I felt pretty good about it.

But the pain remained.
The discomfort did not ease.
Victory so hard fought, never came.

Now I am here, locked up in a Mental Hospital. There are patients who scream like banshees in the night and day.

Others I swear are *Applied Physicists* who study Gravity and Fluid Dynamics. They throw cups of drink and whatever else all over the place.

This morning I happened to catch a surreal glance at an innocent olive-green mug of tea fly past my bedroom door – the tea evacuating the mug as it travelled down the passage. Remarkably, the mug survived! No idea what they're made of, but the Ministry of Defence should grab a few of these to make tank armour from.

The tea, I am saddened to say, was enjoyed solely by the mop. It's really tragic. The poor tea! I mean show me a person who doesn't at least feel the slightest twinge of sadness of *tea* spilt over the floor, and I'll show you a monster...

I jest. Of course. I don't know how to handle situations. Especially unpredictable ones. I mean the tea did spill in the manner described, but I am trying to make light of the traumatic experience by making light of it.

Whilst I care not for my own wellbeing, I feel a deep, profoundly deep amount of empathy for my fellow patients. I look at them at times, and wish with all my being that I had some magic way to help them and fix them. That's been the hardest part of my detention here. Not the fact that I am now "safe" and cannot kill myself, but distress of the patients.

You can see even in their delirious states, that they have this amazingly powerful will to *live,* and carry on living. It's odd to me as I just wish I'd die – I wake up disappointed every morning that I've survived the night. But these poor people who so desperately want to live, damn I wish I could help them.

But I endure.
I keep on existing.
Stupid heart keeps beating.
The stench of my existence lingers.

Don't know why really?

I am in the perfect statistical bracket for dying. I am 44 (2023), have a history of the 80% of the men in my dad's side of the family all died before 50 from heart attacks. I have autism, so suicidally-speaking, I am also in the perfect bracket. In fact, I'd probably struggle to find a single statistic that says I *should* be alive. Hell man, even my dad died when he was 42. I never imagined I'd reach that age, let alone overtake it by now, almost 3 years. And yet, every fucking day, I wake up. Most days, I wake up from nausea.

"Nausea?" you ask.

Yes.

Nausea from pain. Imagine you don't wake up like those stupid TV ads where people wake up so refreshed – but you wake up from nausea due to pain. Most days, to get ready for work, I take a shot of morphine and muscle relaxants (in addition to my 12+ pain tablets) in the morning.

It's no way to *live* man

STOP THE CRAZY TRAIN FOR A MINUTE...

(I tried to anonymise this somewhat, as I don't want to hurt an individual who was an utter arse to me and clearly did not care about me being hurt)

It occurred to me today that people [I've spoken to] don't really know where I am. I mean they get that it's a physical location on a map. They even get that it's a hospital. Some understand that it's a *Mental Health hospital* even. But I don't truly think anyone knows exactly what this place is, and what goes on here. I was sent a sad/ angry text last night from someone I thought loved me, because I (insensitively) described this hospital as an asylum. Actually, it wasn't because of my insensitive description. The person was angry that I don't "Man up" more…

It upset me deeply that I have to carry this individual's trauma and lack of empathy and understanding of what's going on with me – AND FUCKING CARRY MY OWN DEATH-WEIGHT – WHILST BEING HERE. She has her own shit to deal with in life, and I understand that. But I do not see why I should pay for "the sins of the father" and be beaten up emotionally for other people's shit.

Anyway...

I'm not in some lovely hospital in the lush green Welsh hills. OK wait, that's true - that's exactly the setting. The hospital is lovely and the staff are way overdue for a good box of chocolates from me.

I am at this moment, 2 May 2023, 23:41 – carrying Death on my shoulders.
Death is near.
Very.
I can smell Death, I can sense Death.
The measure of my life as of this moment is measured in hours and minutes.
I'm walking on a tightrope above the pit of Death itself

No, this person seems to be under the impression that I'm just in a nice spa retreat, where you see Psychologists and Psychiatrists all the time, sing Kumbaya, and we're all encouraged to have happy-

happy thoughts and turn the frown upside down – *you happy little campers.*

No. No being here is like being handled with a bit of a mild rejection.

You don't get much attention aside from medicine runs – which is good, as I just want to be left-the-fuck-alone. That's not even untrue. On the rare occasion that the Banshee patient does not kick up a racket before 6 am, I am woken by a very friendly nurse for medicine. Mondays and Thursdays, they come get me for Pottery, which I have never done before, but now love.

In the early stages of my incarceration, the staff would come and nag – first that I only ate cheese sandwiches and not even wanting dessert. Now though, later on, they have all accepted that I am quite content with a single cheese sandwich every 2 – 3 days. So most days, if I do not leave my room, I speak to nobody here outside medication 4x per day.

WHICH, I MIGHT ADD, WAS NOT WHAT I WAS TOLD WHEN I WAS SECTIONED!

The main psychiatrist who locked me up in here came to me before I got into the Jail-bulance, and told me to not worry.

Actually, he said *"Don't worry, I am on top of your pain medication. I have a few days off next week, but we're on top of this. We're also going to arrange psychologist and [CBT-type] sessions"*.

Those were his parting words. Pretty much verbatim. Tonight is Friday 12 May. I've seen 2 different psychiatrists who were only doing "Ward Reviews". Nothing else. One did initially take me off Section – kind of – and then the next week the other increased the muscle relaxants I had on my chart.

Other than that, nothing. I ask for some of my Morphine – and sometimes I have to ask an entire day to two days before getting just one dose. I am in so much pain, and I cannot even alleviate it with a hot water bottle, or a hot bath. Just sit here in fairly uncomfortable chairs.

Tonight I'm in the library for the first time. Banshee-lady has been put in here to try safeguard the rest of us, but meant that the library with slightly nicer armchairs was unavailable to the rest of us.

Don't get me wrong, the staff are amazing. I once bought them chocolates (for my first stay), then bought them more chocolates, gift-wrapped and sent anonymously for how amazing they are.

But the Boss-level psychiatrist who promised me, swore to me that he will help me turn the corner on the pain front... he's as absent as mist before the sun, or some other kind of metaphor that means he's not made a single call or appearance in 3 weeks.

No psychologists. No talking therapy. No pain clinic. No fucking painkillers even.

Well, aside from Paracetamol, muscle relaxants and occasional Morphine. F-word, F-word in gerund form, F-word again, I was on nearly fatal doses of medication when I wanted to kill myself to be rid of the pain. Can you imagine how my days are now??

Remember where I initially insulted – attacked – their "ethics"? Yeah, I piss on your vaunted ethics mate. Your Hippocratic Oath starts with *"First do no harm"*. Before you even start doing good, before you even start to consider treatments, DO NOT HARM. I've been harmed in some pretty egregious physical, emotional and psychological ways the last 3 weeks.

Assholes.

WHAT IS IT LIKE IN HERE?
What is a day/week like in the mental hospital?

My experiences of my first, and second admissions were very different. My first admission was "only" a week. The second admission was 5 weeks. I'm not sure that a much longer admission (say 6 months) would be hugely different from the 5 weeks. I'm also not certain that a 2 day admission for example, would be hugely different from the 1 week version.

There's bound to be some redundant information here. I've possibly explained elsewhere, but for ease of reference, I thought I'd create this section and combine all of the day-in-the-life experiences. Having autism myself, change and unknowns are about as comfortable and welcome as a slap in the face with a wet fish (which is not very welcome). If I'd had some idea of what to expect, my trauma going in might have been lessened.

THE DRIVE HERE:
Gosh, this is tough! I thought I'd just write a factual thing, but I am trying to recall the different admissions, and my stomach knots, my spine chills – it's like I am reliving those events in real time!

FIRST ADMISSION:
<u>VEHICLE</u>: Front-wheel drive, manual, diesel engine Ford Kuga. Standard issue as far as I can tell, but with rear child locks enabled. (OH FFS, I just realised the child locks were to keep me in, not the protection of the nurse's children! Bloody hell, I am dim!)

Being a naive moron, I did not know what was happening to me the first time. The psychiatrist very nicely told me that he'd like to book me in to hospital to try out some medication for me. "Fine, I've been in hospital before", I thought. I had this image in mind of being in a "normal" hospital, in a bed – maybe sharing a room with 4 others who have a variety of ailments. I do recall grimacing the first time the psychiatrist mentioned this, and told him I'd not like the noise of being in a room with a bunch of others.

He quickly assured me that I'd be in a room on my own, which calmed me considerably.

The drive to the hospital was weird... I said I'd just drive myself, but they told me that they needed to take me to book me in, and asked me to leave my car keys at Reception, so that my wife can collect the car. They also told me to get my wife to bring me some clothes for the hospital – which she did.

One of the mental health nurses got her car ready, and said that she hoped I wouldn't mind, she had a nursing student who "had to go with her" to the hospital. Not once before, during or even weeks after that trip, did I realise the student did not "need" to go with. She went with to protect the poor nurse in case I turned psycho – but being the ever trusting twat, I never suspected anything. I just took her at face value.

I am such a naive fucking idiot. Believing people who blatantly lie to me. I had no reason to think they'd lie, and honestly would never have harmed her. Why could they not just say "*Oh, look, we're getting Mary-Sue to drive with us as it is standard protocol to have 2 staff in the car*"? That would have been much easier than weeks afterwards figuring out that I was lied to and being a naive moron just believing them.

The actual trip was OK – despite the nurse driving much too slowly and very poorly. I was so anxious about someone getting road rage at the bad driving. But the trip was fine, I chatted to the student and nurse, blissfully unaware of the fact that I was being lied to and really – openly deceived about the whole process!

SECOND ADMISSION:
<u>VEHICLE</u>: Silver Mercedes van. It looked more like a private taxi type deal, than anything NHS-related. The really fun part, was that it had metal mesh on the inside – presumably to stop people escaping/jumping out. The driver was in a totally separate compartment, again I guess to stop patients from assaulting them. I was on the rear bench between one big burly chap and a friendly

woman, with another big guy sat in the bench facing me. The driver was pretty competent, but the damn bench was a nightmare on my awfully sore back.

Ha, what an event that was! See, whilst I was arguing with, and insulting the ethics of the psych-doctors, they had already much earlier that morning, requested a Jail-bulance from Birmingham. In fact, the Jail-bulance had left Birmingham very early the morning – before I had even left home to go to my "appointment".

Looking back at that Monday now, it seems like my admission to hospital was inevitable. I doubt there was anything I could have said that would have made them change their mind – I mean they'd already committed the Jail-bulance crew's (4 people) entire day to transporting me to ~~jail~~ the hospital.

BOOKING INTO HOSPITAL:

En route the first time, I googled the hospital. I found photos of what turned out to be the ancient, now-defunct mental asylum on the grounds. That did little to settle my nerves, as I was filled with dread at being stuck in what looked to be a horrifying place. As I write this, my heart breaks for the poor people who were in mental asylums of old. What horrifying experiences those must have been. My word, I cannot imagine the dread. Doubtless places like that still exist, which just leaves my blood cold.

Anyway, the actual hospital ended up nice enough. We arrived, the friendliest duty manager welcomed us, and took us through a series of locked doors. Again, not realising what I was walking into, I assumed it was just a quirk of the NHS. I was taken to a nice room – room 5.

The mental health nurse and student who drove me there said they had to go "speak to someone" and that was the last I saw of them.

The room was ... austere. A single bed in the middle of the floor, with a chair in the corner. I tried to push the bed to the corner, but it was crazy heavy. The chair equally heavy. Only later did it occur to me that the furniture was all heavy by design, so as to reduce the likelihood of patients picking it up and injuring anyone.

The matron and a nurse then came to my room and asked me to unpack my bags.

By this time, I had been thoroughly overstimulated in the car by feeling that I needed to talk to the driver and passenger, and just wanted some time to get to grips with life. So I politely told the matron that "I'll unpack later".

"No, sorry, we have to unpack with you now, and check what you brought". I then had to unpack absolutely everything, and everything was checked by the matron and the nurse. Checked for weapons, things I can harm myself/others with etc. All my phone cables were confiscated as well as any laptop chargers etc. I tried to protest and say I needed my phone, but NO.

No deal – no exceptions.

Patients MUST have their cables etc locked up in individual lockers, behind locked doors, for which only certain staff had keys.

You could go plug your phone in to charge *and leave it there*, and then hope whenever next the staff are able to open, it's fully charged. But it was very quickly made clear that a phone charging did not take an equal priority with the staff as someone on whose entire existence depended on it. That was hard. I had to just sit in the room. I didn't have anything to read or write with.

The second admission was slightly easier. I knew that they had to check every damn thing I brought with, so I brought fewer items, and fewer cables. I also knew some of the staff by name, which made it slightly easier. *Slightly...*

Oh, and they took all my bags etc, and locked them away. I was literally just left with my clothes and my flat-battery phone.

SUICIDE WATCH

Whilst the matron and nurse finished unpacking my stuff, another lady came in. Different colour and type of uniform. She sat with me for a bit.

By now it was well after 5pm, closer to 6 maybe.

I initially just thought she was there to show me around, but she pulled up a chair and said she'll just sit there, I can do my own thing. After a few minutes, I said "I don't want to be rude, but I'd like to just be alone for a bit". I don't know if it is autism or just my fucked up personality, but I like to be on my own. And after the day I had, I really wanted to just be alone!

Very gently, she said that she had to stay with me. I asked her why, and she said "For safety". A dread filled me, as I imagined a scene from a TV show where prisoners "come to check out the new meat". Shocked, I asked her if there are dangerous people – or something to that effect. She just smiled and said "No, you are on suicide watch". For the next few days, I had to have someone following me everywhere. To lunch, to dinner, while I sleep they had to sit there and even to the toilet I was followed. Not inside the toilet cubicle thankfully, but every 30 seconds or so, she'd call to me and ask if I am OK.

OH! Fuck, is that why I was in room 5? Stupid naive moron.

I thought it was this lovely room all for myself, but I realise only now that it was so they could easier keep an eye on me. The ensuite bathroom had a saloon type door which you could see under and over, allowing minimal privacy for going to the toilet. Damn dude – that is why they had me in there, to keep a better eye on me. Geesh, I am as thick as *whatever a very thick substance is*. How did I not spot this very obvious thing?

Anyway, by I think Thursday I was taken off active suicide watch. But I still had staff come round (both sets of admission) every 5 – 10 minutes to check on me. I eventually learned to live with the lack of privacy, even installing a little LED light above my head so that when

I sleep they could look in on me without needing to come all the way in and switching the very bright main lights on.

TOILET AND SHOWER FACILITIES

How do I not be crass here... I have a great aversion to using public toilet facilities. I can grasp physics. I love Mathematics. I can understand to a degree Quantum Mechanics. But I cannot understand how men have the necessary "equipment" to aim in a toilet, and yet pee all over the place except the toilet bowl. Seriously, HOW?

The problem for me, is that I then go to the toilet after such a pig has been. I'm always worried that someone thinks it was ME who peed all over the place. So I end up cleaning other people's piss off the toilet, just so that people don't think it was me. What a fucking idiot I am – who cleans other people's pee voluntarily? Idiot.

Anyway, that has been a particular issue in hospital. Needing to use the facilities.

An oddity about the facilities, is that the toilet has no seat (probably for "safety"?), but the shower is next to it, so the whole place turns into a "wet room". Cunningly, I have figured out that because of this, the toilet/shower on the right side of the corridor is used less frequently. This has helped me in a number of ways, as I am then able to wash the toilet with soap and hot water before I need to use it. Genius. I have also started carrying hand sanitiser with me, which additionally helps to clean the place.

Room 5 was great for this in my first week, as I had it to myself and I don't mess all over, so at least I had my own clean area. But Room 10 where I am currently shares the facilities. But I've had to (reluctantly) change my entire life to reduce my reliance on the facilities. I eat and drink less, so need the loo less, I shower less often. Not a great solution, but it is a solution...

SHOVELLING FOOD

Food isn't my thing. It really is not. If I had a pill I could take which contained all the nutrients I needed, I'd be happy. I find the whole process of shovelling food down my throat disgusting. And then the toilet afterwards – I mean even at home in my own clean bathroom environment, I find it utterly gross and distasteful.

Food has caused me a LOT of trouble in this place. I really do not want to eat. They have all nice things – salads, main meals, desserts like cakes and custard. You get to choose from a menu what you'd like and it's made for you. For many people (me included), it's more and nicer food than you'd have at home. Even the Sunday Roast that they do is quite an extravagant affair.

At first, they thought I just had cheese sandwiches in order to leave space for desert. But I have been actively refusing even desert, as I really just do not want! Why is that so hard for these people to accept??

Anyway, if you like food, you'll like being here! I cannot speak for ALL NHS Mental Hospitals of course. But even when I was in the spinal hospital for the hydrotherapy treatment for my back, they had lots of fanciful food on offer.

I guess the difference here, is that for some people food is an issue (over/under eating), so they keep a much more strict check on who eats what when.

What I like though, is the very good predictable schedule. A schedule I absolutely do not want to be bound to, but one which my autistic brain likes – the predictability of the whole thing. It feels like it pulls a ring of safety around the day, you know? How odd though that I want the safety and predictability of knowing there's a schedule, but also not wanting to be bound to it. What a weird thing I am.

Every 2 hours you either get food or a warm beverage with biscuits. Not that I ever eat breakfast, but they start with breakfast.

Typical Mealtimes;

6:00 – Warm Beverage with biscuits
8:00 – Breakfast
10:00 – Warm Beverage with biscuits
12:00 – Lunch
14:00 – Warm Beverage with biscuits
15:45 – Warm Beverage with biscuits
17:45 – Dinner
20:00 – Warm Beverage, Sandwiches with biscuits
22:00 – Warm Beverage with biscuits

It is also during these times that most of the friction happen between patients and staff. Makes sense I guess?

You have unwell people who are *forced* to be in a social environment. NO food/warm drinks are allowed in the bedrooms. That was an easy enough calculation for me – I was happy to not eat or drink anything if it meant I had to socialise with others.

The staff eventually started bringing me cheese sandwiches and decaffeinated coffee to my room, as I simply refused to be in a social setting. Reluctantly, I might add. Reluctantly they brought me stuff to my room, as I refuse to leave it.

I forget what I've said and not said, but I have misophonia. Just another part of my delightfully shitty brain where certain sounds set off the monster in me. Particularly eating sounds. Crunching of apples, or slurping tea... You want to see a normally chill man turn into a raging bull within a heartbeat? Slurp porridge next to me... Luckily I've learned to stick my earphones deep into my ear canals to drown out the sound of others eating.

Apparently it is socially unacceptable to dig someone's brain out with a spoon, so I put the music on loud in my earphones instead.

Wait! Why the hell do I even have to pretend I am normal anymore? Damn. I mean I've been locked up by psychiatric professionals – it is quite evident that I am not a normal, healthy human...
Anyway, that is the meal times.

ACTIVITIES

On reflection, I am particularly glad I am not an extrovert.

Being inside this place is a study in loneliness. Even for me, who would be happy to spend day(s) and weeks not talking to anyone, it's lonely. If I so chose, I could sit in my room all day and only have contact with the staff when they bring my medication – and that would be all the human contact I'd have.

There are no group therapy sessions
No sessions to speak to psychologist/professionals about WHY you're here
No sessions to talk to others with similar issues
No sessions to talk about CBT or other ways of coping with life
Nothing.
You just sit there.

It truly is a form of mild neglect.

They just lock you up in a lightly disguised prison cell and now you sit there.

"*Oh, you're here now. Let's check you don't have power cables in your bag. OK, all good. Go sit quietly in the corner*". That sadly seems to not be just my experience, but an experience shared by many fellow patients.

A tragedy and missed opportunity really. It's clearly not the kind of facility you can just pop into. You need medical professionals to *send* you here. Why then do they just abandon you when you get here? Left alone (or with staff if on suicide watch) to sit and mull over your pointless existence without offering any kind of support or anything?

This really is something they can improve on. **Something that SHOULD be improved on!**

They don't need to teach us physics or singing. But maybe every Tuesday and Thursday do mindfulness exercises or breathing techniques, maybe some group CBT lessons. SOMETHING, ANYTHING? Instead of just being left to wallow in misery...

It's partly why I became the useless dick on a donkey – sitting on my mustard yellow chair and being a sounding board for people to come speak to/at. Given the many people who joined me since I started, there's clearly a deep need for someone to be there to talk to.

The staff ARE present, but they have their hands full with patients who sometimes act out, and I cannot fault them on that. But I really feel someone more qualified than old dick here, should be there for people.

In retrospect, they DO have activities though it seems. Sporadic. Sometimes (not often), they have cooking sessions. Someone made a cake one day. But I can understand how there's a lot of risk with allowing one of us to handle knives or boiling liquids, so that makes sense.

One morning, one of the staff popped her head into my room – she's the Activities coordinator. Lovely human. Invited me to go for pottery classes. I was apprehensive, as my only frame of reference for what constitutes pottery classes is what I've seen on TV. Lumps of clay going funny on the wheel thing.

But this ended up being only a small part of Pottery – and not at all something offered here. We sit on normal chairs around a normal table and each get a lump of clay.

Pottery

Depressed, the potter holds the clay -
A beautiful lump of clay!
Every lump, formless as it is,
brims with infinite potential;
Every lump transforms into Unique

A cold lifeless lump -
Takes on life with every breath of the clueless potter -
His first creation, his first touch of clay;
The potter's hands obeys the form hidden in the clay

Every crease and fold brings it to life
Slowly the beauty that was hidden
Shines through more and more
In the end, turns out to be its own unique self
Elated, the potter admires the exquisite and unique

I've loved the pottery.

It was so incredible sitting there in the lazy autumn sun, quietly with a group of others. Our minds focused on the clay in our hands, thoughts drowning in chaos elsewhere, fixed firmly on the warmth of the cold clay in our hands. Free from cultural expectations of creating something "great" – we each get lost in the silence and comfort of the cold clay.

There are other activities – some "mindfulness", but nothing like what I alluded to earlier. They are more informal and few join the sessions.

Another nice thing is that patients who appear more ... "normal"? are invited to go to the shop runs. A nice opportunity to see the outside world at a slower pace, maybe get a few things from the shop. I just stay inside – even if I am allowed out, my agoraphobia prefers being inside. Safe.

There are other things like board games and newspapers to read. I particularly enjoyed the Scrabble. The facilities coordinator has regular quiz sessions which a few regulars attend. But they're more like drop-in sessions rather than scheduled things. The autistic part of my brain kinda wishes that they were all scheduled. Not to necessarily join them, but more for the safety of being able to predict them.

Oh, and there's a TV. *eye roll* It's hidden behind wood and toughened glass, and people who are not me are in charge of the remote control. So sometimes you end up being flooded by the poor content, or loud volume – or both – of whatever whoever deemed appropriate to have on.

Only, there was once that the TV remote was dropped by a staff member who had to go attend an emergency, so I took the liberty of going to the menu, hooking the TV up to my phone's universal remote control. That ensured bliss (for me at least), as I was able to turn the overly loud volume down during meal times or when we tried to play Scrabble and nobody was watching the very loud whatever BBC-show.

Thank goodness for technology!

But it really was in the library that I have been able to find the greatest solace. As I found throughout my school life, the library was a haven, a sanctuary of peace and silence. The loud, obnoxious kids never went in there, and it was a paradise of books to read. Not that there's a great deal of books here, but it's been nice to have a quiet place to sit and write.

Of course, there's a quad which is surrounded by the main building and what must be a 4 metre-tall wall. Patients go there mostly to smoke, but also get some "fresh air" (cigarette-filled). Some kick the football, some sit and chat or have exercise sessions. For me, I only go out late at night before the door is locked, or when it rains. Then I get to walk out there alone, without needing to choke on cigarette smoke.

But that's about all there is in terms of "activities" – like I said, this place is a study in loneliness.

The Activities Coordinator is amazing. She makes a lot of effort to engage patients – this is aside from things like a bit of pottery or cooking. We play Scrabble on occasion, do some quizzes or colouring.

BEDROOMS

I think I previously said the bedroom is spartan or austere. You have a single bed on a super heavy base, thin mattress, in a plastic-ish type cover. Presumably for easy clean?

The sheets and blankets are utilitarian. Given my first stay was in early Spring, I was cold often. Pillows were in short supply, but they gave me a few extra to help support my neck.

My wife brought my fleece blanket from home – but it took a shit-load of begging and pleading to allow even that! They don't allow much of our shit from home. I could not even bring my Optimus Prime from home to "keep me company". Though I was allowed to buy a "heavy fluff toy" (a dog) to keep me company. I missed having a pet with me, and I missed my Oodie weighted blanket from home. The heavy fluff toy made for a soothing weight. Still, some consideration could be given to people with neurodiversity issues.

 I mean, you have mentally unwell patients in here. Some, like me, who were/are desperately suicidal. So they lock me/us in here, then neglect us. For Real? DUDE! FUCK man. Anyway… That's the bedroom bit.

They did eventually allow me a solar charger (which could wirelessly charge my phone) which saved me the enormous frustration of begging to charge my phone in the locked laundry room. I get why they insist on locking away chargers – patients could strangle themselves and others. But in light of the utter lack of anything else to do, they could make charging our electronics easier.

Again, that speaks to the mild neglect we're treated with here (aside from a few staff members who are outright hostile!)

MEN VS WOMEN

It's always interesting how people perceive the world, based on their own various character traits and bias. Take me for example. It would be a stretch for me to go through the day where I didn't analyse *something*. Except for people that is. But here, with the lack of much else to analyse, I have been paying a lot of attention to the patients.

I've been here now over 2 weeks. I've seen various patients of both genders come and go. Mostly, the gender split is a pretty even 50/50. The most interesting thing has been how much more violent the women are.

Considering the almost 50/50 split, out of 8 women, 4 are needing restraints, and staff within an arm's reach at all times. One of those needs 3-4 staff around her all the time. So it's fair to say that at least 50% of the women are given to frequent violent outbursts of anger. That ranges from shouting, slamming doors repeatedly, to getting into some very physical altercations, needing "special" care. One in particular frequently throws things – mugs full of tea, empty mugs, books, board games – I mean everything, anything

The men on the other hand are pretty chill. There's one who is "excitable", but on balance seems fairly solid, and expecting to be released soon. Another guy walks up and down the passage all day with a gait not unlike that of a zombie. But every now and then he uses his head to (try) open the very well sealed doors. Literally. He runs into the doors with his head. So he permanently has a bandaged head.

So there are... "incidents" with the men. But they seem very focused on harming themselves, and only themselves.

The women at times get riled up and, a number of them would join the fray, necessitating the special nurse alarm, which gets all the staff on deck to help calm things. Maybe they just stick together?

Obviously this is by no means scientific or significant – it's just an interesting thing I've noticed

---

Interlude

The Zombie walk is one thing most people here have in common (me included I think).

~~We...~~
They all walk with this slow zombie-like gait that is just so sad. You can tell the *truly* unwell people from the others. The truly unwell walk with said zombie-like gait that appears they have no hope, no future, no life. They've literally become walking corpses that just... exist. Exist to survive the hours between meal times. Exist to survive the hours between sleep and awake and in between those hours, they just walk like the Romero's Zombies.

Very depressing!

We can dive the deepest seas. We can send robots to other planets and we can probe the deepest mysteries of the Universe. *But we seem unable to cure mental health issues.* Even Physical health is relatively easily treated – routinely even. But mental health seems to be the one thing that we can mask with pills. We can gloss over it in ways using pretend techniques, but really, it seems that we cannot truly *cure* it.

I'm not talking here about occasional sadness, or even bouts of Seasonal Affective Disorder (SAD). I'm talking true mental health issues that I see other patients and myself exhibit here.

Psych doctors would of course disagree. But I remain convinced that we will never be able to cure mental illness

CHAIRNESS

Plato, I believe, came up with the concept of "Chairness". At least, I think it was Plato. Guess I could check, but what good is vaunted intellect if you cannot even remember things like who came up with Chairness?

Anyway, Chairness basically refers to the ability of someone to be able to look at something they don't necessarily specialise in, or have great technical knowledge on, and know it's not right.

The argument was that a person would not have to be a specialist carpenter or craftsman who specialises in making chairs, to know if a chair is good or not.

Even if a person doesn't know a chisel from a file, they would be able to tell you that if a chair has 4 different length legs, or just 2 legs, or no base to sit on, it is no good. They don't need to be experts. You just instinctively know, given Life's Experience.

Take a heart surgeon for example;

They train for many years to become surgeons. But if they did a heart transplant and attached the new heart to your right knee, you would damn well be able to say "That's not how it works mate".

So applying Chairness to mental health is the same concept. Locking me up in this fucking place for week(s) is not right. It's not how I think mental health should be addressed - especially with the levels of mild neglect and borderline hostility I've picked up on.

What's the answer? Don't fucking know. But it's not this.

Besides, I have a pain issue. I lie awake so many damn nights, in agony from my spine.

But there is something else wrong with me. I do not know what. I have a complete inability to mingle with and understand human interaction. I struggle profoundly on a daily basis in every form and type of interaction with people. And no, I'm not demon possessed you bloody arsehole. It's something else.

You know how in The Matrix movie, Neo sees the green Matrix code when he faces off with the agents at the end? That's how I feel. I can see the green code of Life. But there is something else. Code that's written in a different colour, using a different language.

There's something else wrong with me, which gives a symptom of mental health, but it's more of a profound misunderstanding of Life. Imagine taking your petrol powered car and putting diesel in. There's nothing wrong with the car itself (well until you drive it with the wrong fuel). But it's something else. Something that causes its engine to not function with the input.

Like the Matrix. A fault in my code. I feel it. It's life a sneeze in the back of my brain. I'm certain there's something neurological that can probably account for why I am so broken, aside from just brushing it off as depression.. I wish I knew what that was...

ESCAPE IS A GLASS PANE AWAY

I held my hand against the cold double-glazed glass next to my ugly chair the other day.

So amazing that such a thin, fairly fragile, glass pane can hinder my escape.

There's a poem about it in my head I think – my brain just needs thinking space. After 15mg Zopiclone, there's a very steady, rapid downward trend in available creative neurons still at their posts... But I think a poem is writing itself in my subconscious.

But what a day it was!

I "made" a table of peace and safety where I've had a number of patients come to just sit quietly without feeling the need to talk. Or they can talk if they want.

I just keep it a safe zone.

It's pretty scary. I just sit there feeling vulnerable, open for anyone and everyone to come speak to or at. Pretty damn frightening, but it seems like the kind of thing my fellow patients need.

But there is this one patient has been like a raging bull, wrecking everything, and throwing stuff around, drooling on things like your phone or table, so that's not awesome. Actually, I feel sorry for her. I previously described her as Banshee-lady. Which was unkind. The more I study her, the more my heart breaks for her. Fuck. What a monster I am. To call someone who is in such distress a banshee. It does not matter that I only later found out how troubled she was. The point is I judged her before knowing it. I am a fucking cruel monster.

But the general idea is – given that I don't think I have a mental illness – to create a zone where people can talk to someone who is fairly coherent. I mean there's nothing else to do here, and the staff are so damn busy all the time. Occasionally they would chit-chat to us. But for the majority of the time, they don't seem to have time (or interest) to engage beyond the surface.

Still, one or two seem pretty caring. One nurse (doctor?) is from the Caribbean and her and I have had a few nice conversations. A couple of the other nurses are very sweet. One is so full of sunshine – she lights up a room. She talks to people with such a lovely tone. Another one (black hair to remind myself who she is), seems more … serious(?). No, that's not the right word. Don't know the right word – but she's not immediately obviously outgoing and loud. But she has such a beautiful caring nature about here. (Edit; she's the one who came to tell me I have to eat, and monitored me at the "Anorexia table")

DICK ON A DONKEY

My boys have an unfair advantage in life, and I am not even sorry. For I gave them something – withheld rather – that most take for granted. What is this thing I withheld, you may ask. Good question.

Fairy tales

Never taught them any fairy tales. They don't know the story of Rosamund and the 7 pigs, or Imogen and the sleeping prince. None of that. Even as week-old babies, instead of lullabies or night time stories, I taught them physics, and science and stuff like drag coefficients and the Schwarzschild radius. I mean they were now alive, and young though they were, their brains were ready to start taking on information. Not once did I tell them the story of the Lion and the Wolf...

...*On an unrelated note*, they were both very hard to get to sleep during their first weeks-months on the planet. No idea why.

Anyway – weird intro to this chapter.

As you might have guessed, I don't actually know any fairy tales. I'm sure I was taught them as a child, I was always more interested in facts rather than stories, because I hated that the rabbits were so stupid to let the wolf in just because it had flour on its foot. Or was it pigs?

One pernicious lie most parents tell their children though, is the lie about the "*Knight in shining armour*". **Filthy, pernicious, wretched lie**.

Think about it. Knight in shining armour? ABSOLUTELY NO KNIGHT WHO WAS IN BATTLE, RETURNED FROM BATTLE IN SHINING ARMOUR. Those who survived the field of battle were bloodied, bruised, sweat mixed with dirt and blood clinging to every piece of exposed skin, and armour equally filthy, bent and broken.

THOSE were the Knights. Those to me were the true knights – the ones who had been tested in battle. The ones who took their swords in their hands, and did violent things to evil men in order to keep their loved ones and country safe. Those are the heroes. Those are the ones I learned too late in life to look up to for inspiration.

I use the word *pernicious* here with intent. The stupid, false tale of a knight in shining armour being the hero has for too long set men for the most part, up to fail. Those of us who do not cower in the face of evil are bloodied and bruised. We fail a parry, and our swords are knocked to the ground. We are knocked to the ground. And time, after time, we pick up our swords again – with ever dwindling strength – just so that we can try ward off just one more blow against our loved ones.

Many of us lose the fight. Many of us die on the field of battle, in service and sacrifice to those we love.

Trust me. Over the last 2 months, I have become intimately familiar with the statistics behind the rates of suicide – especially among men. Whilst a larger portion of women *attempt* suicide, men are more likely to be successful. More lethal. For various reasons, which I may or may not go into later, but suffice to say that there is a lot of statistical data that backs up my assertion. Men are disproportionately, negatively, affected by suicide.

Anyway. Some of us for reasons unknown, did not have the honour to die on the field of battle. Some of us survive by chance, or divine appointment, or just sheer fucked up "luck".

So we return home.

To the victor the spoils.

But to the losing team, nothing but humiliation, shame and failure. Bringing shame and dishonour to our names and families. It would have been better to have died that day, whatever day, than to return home like this. Some of those who return, the mighty captains, return on their mighty steeds and regardless of victory or defeat, are welcomed Home. Given rest. Healed. Banquets thrown just to celebrate their return.

Proud Knights, worthy of the title. Armour battered and bruised though it may be, are held up as proud battle scars – worthy of remembrance.

Then there are the ... "knights" like me. Useless footmen really.

The Dick on a Donkey.

That's me.

The *nobody* who wasn't much use on the field of battle, couldn't walk home because he's too weak, finally able to trap an innocent donkey to return home on, burdening the poor beast. Not through the Glorious City Doors – just kind of sneak in through the ivy-covered back gate next to the water mill in the dead of night. Shame too great, courage too absent to even face those whom you failed. Sword broken or lost because you're damn inept. Worthy of nothing but death in the face of defeat.

Frankly, it's probably one of the things I despise MOST about myself. If I had the ability to plug a computer cable into my brain, this would be the one thing I'd change; *To stop always trying to be the heroic knight who tries to help people.* To realise, once and for all, that I am just the dick on a donkey – Stop trying to help you stupid fuckwit. Fuck, you annoy me. Fucking irritates me. Why do I keep wanting to help people? Fucking moron.

Take my stay in this hospital. Elsewhere (and I am too lazy and frustrated with Bluetooth mouse nonsense to check), I probably wrote in some contrived, self-important way about how I try help people here.
Trying to help by being a "*quiet voice*" I think is the phrase I used. Or giving people access to my personal WiFi hotspot because the hospital's WiFi is garbage.

I have given a number of people my personal hotspot information to access as they want, without limit, so that they can also enjoy internet as I do. As if it matters.

What horse shit
As if that matters to these people at all.

People are probably just glad to get online, the fact that I am the *dick on the donkey* to give them access to internet is hardly of measure in any kind of scale. But there I was just earlier tonight, not only giving a new patient my hotspot details, but also offering unlimited use of my wireless solar battery pack.

We're not allowed cables in our rooms, so for the more tech-savvy, capable patients, it is an enormous frustration to go leave their devices to charge in the laundry while they charge. But hey, not to worry – *dick on the donkey* is here to help save the day. Now you can charge your iPhone in your room for 2 consecutive days without needing to go to the lockup to charge. As if it matters where they charge their stuff. You know?

But hey, the useless dick on the donkey is ever ready, ever willing to help, just to prove he's not a total waste of oxygen.

You know, I look at the great men of history at times and in vain try understand why and how they were so great. It's not even that I really want to be "great" at this point. Just not *entirely useless* would be a good start.

I guess this is why I am here – because I realised my use, and it was little.

So the only rational choice ~~was~~ is to, *before* coming home in defeat and shame *again*, fall on my sword. At least that way, my loved ones can live under the delusion that I fought and died, just like great men one hundred-fold my worth.

Dick on a Donkey

Equus asinus;
You poor innocent beast
One moment a carefree ass
At once burdened by an arse
I'm sorry I burden you!

The innocent donkey awoke,
Amongst fresh green grass
Water so sweet, without a yoke
Yet now embarrassed under my lazy arse

I'm a failed knight with no honour;
Amour broken
Sword shattered
shield bloodied
King's banner lost in mud

Utterly disgraced, I try head home
Weak
broken
Cowardly
dishonoured
I afflict the donkey like a virus

Too humiliated to show my face
I ride to town in the night
I'm not a worthy knight
My failures too great to walk in light
Enter through the sewer to hide my disgrace

Victorious knights feasting
Jesters jesting
Jubilant dancing
King's toasting
Through shitty sewers I sneak in

Discard my broken armour!
Burn my name!
Become a peasant!
I deserve neither name nor life
Between us, the donkey has more honour

So crawl back into the hole
Vaunted former knight;
Weighed
Measured
Wanting
The poor donkey is your greater

A last act before I depart into the night;
Donkey - I set you free
My gift a bag of crunchy carrots
Escape to your fresh pasture
Enjoy your sweet co water
I'm sorry I tainted you
A dishonourable worthless knight

DETECTIVE MILLER

You know, I remember dumb things I did as a child - like playing "Ninja tricks" with my dad's rain gauge aged 12. I remember the Thursday clearly – had a Sport Day at school, and I came home all charged up with energy. It was a sunny day, and having seen a Bruce Lee movie a couple of weeks prior, decided to re-enact the movie (such as I recalled) outside. I got hold of an old broom stick we had lying around, and used that as my bo-staff.

After laying waste to the evil ninjas (weeds) in my mother's flower bed, all that was needed, was to take down the Boss. Without a clearly defined Boss in the backyard, the only evil-ish figure I could identify was my dad's upside-down pyramid-shaped rain gauge. After performing some stunning acts and tricks (moves) and whacking the poor rain gauge from a number of angles, I swung round for the final blow.

It occurred to me an hour later, as I watched the hands of doom on the clock march to my father's home time, that I was an utter moron. Cowering in the corner, I tried to figure out a plausible excuse for the rain gauge's demise in order to not get a hiding from my dad. The man never used tools, always his hand for hidings. But man, he used to hit me that I pissed myself and any socks, shoes and carpet that was in the way.

Point is, I remember dumb things I did as a kid. I guess most people do? Only I seem to get caught in an inescapable gravity well of memories I cannot escape, and end up ruminating. I still often cuss at myself for doing the exact dumb things I did as a child, and then wonder how in the hell 32 years have passed and I still do the same stupid shit. Though I can safely say that I have not destroyed a rain gauge in years

BUT!

As I sit here tonight, I realise that I have grown in many respects. Perhaps my all out, self-hatred isn't entirely warranted for my apparent shortcomings in life.

Take TV shows, movies, books etc for example; I have all my life looked up to/held in esteem the Leader. The heroic, sacrificial leader who wins the day, free from any blemishes or shortcomings. The figurative knight in shining armour.

But the older I've become – and dude, this is literally the last 4 years or so really – I've started to sway away from that clichéd perfect leader, and found myself... Well, not quite rooting for the villains, but certainly understanding the more complex, "grey", conflicted characters more. I guess it is after my ever-perfect self image was slowly and carefully shattered night, after agony-filled night since my back injury. The less-than-perfect characters have become the ones I look to. Maybe not always for guidance really, but also to know that it's OK to not be the messiah in the show.

I've also especially started loving characters that make me feel normal. I don't want to use the nauseating "representation" word here. But there are certainly characters on TV and movies that I look to in order to feel normal. I see their behaviour and thoughts and I think "Ah yea, I am not the miscreant after all, others also feel/think like this". Take for example shows like Dexter. Dexter is someone I love watching, as he really makes me feel so normal. It's like hearing my own inner dialogue from the TV speakers. It is wonderful. Not the killing bit though... Just if you were wondering.

All of this finally brings me back to the heading title; Detective Miller. A man who is a bit of a complex case, is introduced in the TV show Expanse. One slightly humorous incident is when Miller showers, shampoo all over his head and bam! His shower is cut short. Out of water. Water quota exceeded.

The rest of the story is interesting for context, as I have experienced in ~~prison~~ hospital what Detective Miller experiences when showering. It was weird tough, and unexpected. I've found that I am able to just start showering and left with a lot of soap in my hair as the water ration, So I learned to first wash my hair in the basin, rinse in the basin water allocations, then soap. Once all of that is done, I get under the severely timed shower to flush off the last soap parts.

Feels just like that episode that Miller had!

THE SHITTY FORK IN THE ROAD

You always have choices in life.
Remember that.
It's a great lie that people tell themselves "I had no choice".

'Course you do. It's just that you've already – subconsciously maybe – discounted the shitty ones. Take work for example. You have a choice to work or not. Nobody really forces you. Not even if you worked for drug lords. The option to stop selling drugs might well mean they kill you – but *that's still a choice you make*. I frankly cannot honestly think of a single situation in life that you don't have a choice (other than being born). It's just that the options and the ramifications of one of the other choices are unpalatable to you. But the choice is very much there.

People need to realise this deep truth more frequently – it is very liberating.

So *Emo*-Nico stands at a pretty shitty fork in the road. As far as I can tell with my apparently messed up head, I have 2 options;
Keep existing.
Or
Stop existing.

Carrying on existing – which is what I tried so desperately to get the psychiatrists to understand – is not an option I relish. I have lived through almost 5 years of hell. Where even the good, joyful moments – such as they were – were marred by pain and discomfort. A striking reminder that the pain will never end, no matter how "good" things get.

The frankly profound struggle of trying to hold down a pretty senior role, filled with technical complexity and pressure, whilst in constant pain, and fighting the sedative effects of painkillers is a bit of a bastard.

Taking a lower paying job is one of the aforementioned choices in life. I decided against it, as I measure my worth to society by the tax I pay and the tangible cash value I bring to my community.

I'm an analyst.
I measure and analyse things.

As far as I am aware, nobody can measure their value to society at large through "just being there" or "being a good friend". *Dafaq* does that even mean?

How many Pounds Sterling is being a *good friend* worth? £1.83 per day? £388.11 per month? £1k per year? Does being a "best friend" mean you're worth 50% more? If you have 2 friends, are you worth £1.83 per day for each? Or is it like tax where you're only worth £1.83 per day for the first friend, £1.50 for the second, and then £0.91 per friend thereafter?

Does taking out your neighbour's garbage add £100 per month to your worth in society? Does mowing the lawn for Mrs Best up the road add £25 per month?

HOW. THE. HELL. DO. YOU. QUANTIFY. THIS???

How do you quantify friendship? How do you quantify your worth as a human? It's a self-evident fact that, as you look at society at large, as well as individual humans, many have zero idea how to measure their worth. It's been my personal observation that humans are very poor estimators of their own worth. The really shitty humans who treat others terribly often hold themselves in high esteem. Conversely, those who are the true gems of society, people we need more of in the world, are often the ones who either struggle to measure their own worth, or calculate it at a very low end of the scale.

Except me of course. Being the observer in this scenario, I am very uniquely qualified to measure my own worth. Which with a salary is pretty low, and now without a salary is near zero. Maybe less than zero.

But paying £30,000 in taxes per year – *that is quantifiable*! That means something, you know? At least in my own (apparently) messed up estimation. It means I am paying more in taxes than what I earned as a pizza shop manager. It means that my worth to society is greater. Not my social standing mind you – just the value that the money I earn in terms of helping fund hospitals, or build schools etc. It means I'm allowed to exist quietly in some dark corner.

I don't say this to be boastful. I am saying it because I am so desperate to feel like I am allowed to exist on this planet. And I can think of no other way to justify my continued existence. Because if I am not contributing financially, my worth is nil.

As for social standing, really don't care for it. I remember in 2019, I had to fly to the Philippines for work. The company paid for a business class ticket on Cathay Pacific. WHAT AN EXPERIENCE! It was so cool – the novelty I mean. But what was so bizarre, is how people bowed to your every whim. As if you are suddenly better than the person sitting in Economy, 8 rows behind you.

Actually, on that flight from Manchester to Hong Kong, something truly bizarre happened. One of the 4 very luxurious Business Class toilets had some or other "malfunction". So the duty service manager came to each of the Business Class passengers individually, and gave us each a $150 voucher as apology and compensation. As if! Dude, I'll just go to the other toilets. But no, apparently we were too good for that, and got said voucher. NO WAY would the Economy passengers get that.

Point is, it made me feel very uncomfortable to be treated like that. Like I am somehow better than other people.

Besides, I've always much preferred to sit and have a great lunch with the cleaning staff than the "big wigs". Heck, most of my happiest lunches at work were with the cleaning crew. No pretence, no bullshit. In Cape Town, I was a lecturer in a college that catered largely to under-privileged students. We used to every Friday go to the Fish & Chips shop on the ground floor. We'd buy chips and sausage and bread and a bunch of students and I would call *Auntie Minnie* the cleaner and share the lunch with her. We had such great laughs and shared stories over shared bread and chips.

Whereas the most awkward lunches have been with the "big wigs" in restaurants that provide more cutlery for one person than I own. With "food" on the menu that I could hardly pronounce, and never being sure if I must sit, salute or prostrate in reverence.

JOB INTERVIEWS

Chances are if you read this, you are probably aware of how stressful it can be to apply for jobs. You know how applying for jobs can be even more stressful?

TRY APPLYING FROM INSIDE A MENTAL HOSPITAL! Geesh.

The exhaustion of trying to pretend you're OK, trying to pretend you really give a damn about a culture and history of a company that's merely number 713 in the number of jobs you've applied for – *that is exhausting.*

Then doing the phone interviews whilst 2 patients are attacking each other and one is throwing cups of tea past your window! Wow. Your "Mute call" game better be on top form. All this would have been worthwhile though, *if every fibre of your being did not yearn to die...*

Well, actually though – despite everything I've said, I don't think I *truly* want to die. I just want to be free from this paralysing pain. Is there not maybe a road less travelled that means getting rid of the pain, and then being able to *live?* Wish there were...

Don't laugh. We can all fantasise, can't we?

THE ROAD TO RECOVERY

It seems on balance that I am not currently on the road to dying. But I'd hesitate to call it the road to recovery though. The psychiatrists merely think they hit the Pause button. I'll let them live with that delusion for now – feels like I am toying with them like a cat toys with a mouse

Recovery would first of all mean that I'd have to go through the incredible effort of revisiting and rewriting my entire value system and to believe that I am somehow of value to society without it involving a salary!

Recovery would mean that my back isn't frakked up and I can look forward to a life. I recall looking at a preacher as he got up to do a sermon once. He was 66 at the time – I heard his age and quietly, under my breath just prayed "Please God, no". As in NO, don't ever let me live that long. The bitter irony here, is that at that time, I wasn't even suicidal, I wasn't even injured back then!

Recovery would mean a lot of things that I am not truly convinced I am capable of.

Not convinced I want actually.

When you've lived with chronic pain this long, as bad as this, it is hard to imagine a future that isn't laced with pain. I'd have greater ease to believe aliens existed, or Bigfoot exists or any host of other things – I'd believe any of those before I'd believe I can exist without pain. It's just been such an awful, perverse experience.

I don't even know what such a life could look like.

Then of course, there's the fact that over the last 5 years, I've had over 1,200 pills per month and over 29 litres of morphine. I'd imagine my liver is pretty fucked, and I'm due for a death from cirrhosis anyway! A long, painful one at that. I truly cannot see why I can't just switch off the lights now?

FUN INTERLUDE (Sunday 30 April, 2023, 20:42 – the Common Room):
Maybe I will do occasional interludes to save people my drama.

So around 8pm (and other times), a shutter – a damn loud shutter – is opened up, and coffee, tea and sandwiches are handed out. Your first mistake would be thinking that these events go by without incident.

I recall the first time I ventured out of my room to get bitter tea, one of the patients was absolutely adamant to have a 3rd cup of milk. Her requests were denied. WOW, how the cups of pre-poured tea and biscuits flew through the air as her temper raged! And honestly, I cannot fathom how the 3rd cup of milk would have been worse than the tea and biscuits she made airborne. In a financial calculus, the milk seems like a pretty petty sacrifice. But then, I've already illustrated how I don't "get" humans, let alone the rules in this place.

Back to tonight.

Sitting on my ugly mustard yellow chair, writing this. One of the patients whom I had built a pretty good rapport with came in, chatting ever so loudly. He was out on day leave, and I overheard one of the nurses give him hell over having caffeine drinks (everything we have is super-decaf, for obvious reasons). Anyway, another much younger patient (about 20 I guess) who arrived the day after me – also in for a month – ventured out of his room. Clearly never grew up in the wilds of Africa where you are taught to *not challenge whoever thinks they're the Alpha, by looking them square in the eyes*. As a self-identified Sigma Male (LOL), I know this and honestly the whole pissing-the-deck-with-testosterone doesn't phase me. In my eyes, the whole Alpha male territorial bullshit is just tragic and pitiful.

But this poor young buck made some comment that I didn't catch, which set our Alpha off, and they nearly came to blows, with the

young buck refusing to apologise, or stop staring at the Alpha in challenge. It is remarkable how quickly things can escalate – especially in a setting where nobody has anything in common, other than a mental health issue!
That's the story. Nothing happened.

Not giving a damn about the whole "my ego is bigger than your dick" thing, I tried to defuse the situation and told the young buck to look at his sandwich. The momentary break in eye contact was enough to break the dick waving and tension.

Honestly, why the hell am I here?
There's absolutely NOTHING wrong with me. I feel like such a fraud

DAY-WHATEVER

I don't even know what damn day it is anymore. OK, I looked at my phone, it is Friday. I slept until after 1pm today. Then reluctantly dragged myself upright.

It's fair to say the will to live has pretty much left me. I skipped breakfast and lunch. Wanted to write a bit, but alas the hospital was running half an hour late with food, so I almost ended up in the Common Room with the other patients.

Last night, I had some tuna with my cheese sandwich. I HATE tuna. I only had it, as one patient was eating so messily, that he spat out tuna he was eating onto my cheese sandwich and I didn't realise until it was too late.

Monday this week, the staff had purchased some sugar-free lemonade. They gave us some with dinner, then left the bottle at the water fountain. I had some of it on Monday. Tuesday also had some. Tuesday evening, I saw one of the patients pick up the bottle... and she drank straight from the damn bottle. UNBELIEVABLE. I felt sick to my stomach. Fuck man

Since then, I've become a recluse. I don't leave my room except for dire need. Staying inside. I am in a lot of pain day and night.

The psychiatrist has reviewed my meds, made some marginal changes, but beyond that, I have to keep existing in pain until mid-next week when the main psychiatrist/GP comes back from leave to review my medication.

FUCK.

I just wish the damn pain would end.

My mind is La Brea

A visceral hellscape;
Like the tar pits of La Brea
My mind's become a prison
Torture day and night
How to escape I've no idea

Like an animal trapped in the tar
I'm stuck in unending torment
No reprieve in sight
In the light of day or dark of night

La Brea!
The tar pit of my mind holds me captive
The more I struggle
The tighter it holds
To escape the torment
I have only one final idea

Sleep brings no solace
Daylight brings more sorrow
I'm engulfed by the tar
My only prayer that there's no tomorrow

HEALTH UPDATE WHATEVER

What is the date... Dunno man. Somethingth of May.

Wednesday 3 May 2023 – the psychiatrist has reviewed my condition. He's removed my Section. Not sure why. The removal of the Section is also not exactly 100% removed. It's kinda removed. I'm now back to being "informal". This means that I could, if I wanted to, leave the premises after notifying the staff. But there are limits, I cannot go to Hawaii for example.

My wife is coming to visit tomorrow with a friend – on the king's Coronation. Naughty peasants ☺

Looking forward to the visit. It'll be nice to see them and leave the premises a bit.

Trouble is, I have to come back! I cannot leave and stay...left. Stay away. I have to come back, or they will fetch me and then the gloves come off. So I will play nice.

Watching the movie Greenland as I write this. I love the music. Morena Baccarin's character is an utter cow though. That pressed-lip look she gives John when she *orders* him to go get beer and stuff – I can see why that relationship went awry. People don't realise how men (most men) are put off when they are disrespected like that.

Anyway. SO health update. No longer under Section. Not entirely certain I give a shit. I'm literally just sitting here waiting for the email result of the job interview. Since I made that my Go/No-Go trigger, I have to wait to get the result.

But the thought of spending another 2 weeks to 6 months in this place is *rather unappealing*. QUITE unappealing.

THE PEACH PIT

In this document somewhere, I referred to suicide as a peach pit I chewed thoroughly. The analogy meaning I carefully thought it through. Carefully. Even if the pain is removed *right now,* even if I got a whatever job, at the end of the day, I am ageing and my body will eventually become frail. A lot of shitty things lie ahead as a natural cause of ageing.

Kinda makes sense to just draw the line under this story now whilst I still can. There are people who go through all manner of horrendous situations in life where they are incapable of looking after themselves. The hell am I ever going to accept an existence where that is acceptable.

They've already lost

They run the marathon
They compete in the sport
They play the game

Make every sincere effort
Deliver only their best
Use every ounce of concentration

Yet they've already lost

A day, week or year ago
The smallest decision
Long determined their result

They just don't know, they've already lost

In my game about living on Mars
Colonists work and strive
Sadly in a month, none will be alive

Crops early on failing, they just don't know they're already dead

So many in life live in bliss
Every warning sign is a miss
Innocent, Ignorant - they've already lost

CORONATION DAY – 6 MAY 2023

Well... Coronation Day...

When I arrived here on Monday 24 April, the staff had some bunting and Union Flags out that needed to be painted/decorating in preparation for today. One of the nurses very excitedly asked if I am going to be here for Coronation Day and if I wanted to decorate some bunting.

Her excitement at "*Oooh, you are going to be with us for the Coronation then*" was like a dagger of ice that pierced my heart, and froze my blood. I just smiled outwardly, but in my soul I was screaming like a prisoner thrown into a cold, dark dungeon. I even, on that same intake day, decided to protest/whatever the fancy word is (appeal?), against my incarceration. I never in my darkest dreams, thought I'd be here still by today. And yet, here I am. Fuck.

I mean, if things that you could not in your darkest dreams imagine happen, I dare not look into the abyss of the horrors that life can truly throw at you!

Anyway... I got job news today. The news didn't catch me – what caught me out was the *reaction* I had to the news. The company gave *very positive* feedback, and wants to arrange a 2nd stage interview. Now I have to stay my hand until after then.

It's weird

So many people who *want* to live, even here where there are patients so unwell that they are barely "present" and even they have this deep inner fire (so it seems) to live and survive. Even a couple of the new patients who came in and spoke to me, spoke about how they reached out for help.

Meanwhile, I seem to be the only one sitting with a bucket of water, ready to pour it over my little fire to extinguish it.

Indeed, a little disappointed that I, by my own agreement with myself, now have to wait and continue existing until after the 2nd round of interviews.

But still, I disagree profoundly with the GP and Psychiatrists that I have a mental disorder. What I *do have*, is a physical disorder, one which I am rather desperate to escape. I wish the doctors could grasp this.

Take this morning; I woke up from the emergency alarm because the one patient was awake early and made a heck of a ruckus. But I happened to be surfacing by 6am (2 hours before my alarm), because of damn pain. Felt nauseas from the damn pain. *That is my disorder.* A physical one.

<u>But isn't it Psychosomatic?</u> (I think the phrase was Psychogenic Pain)

POP QUIZ; How do you know you're an insensitive asshole? You suggest to someone that the hell they're going through is merely in the mind. Maybe they're just stressed out a bit, and if they go to a weekend zen- or hippie-weed-smoking retreat, they'll feel all better. Or just needing anti-depressants.

Because yeah, you know, someone is awake day and night from pain – but is just imagining it because he's a bit stressed out. Fucking yuppie that cannot cope with a bit of stress.

Because yeah, you know, someone sweats from the agony and pain they're in – but hey ho, just pop this anti-depressant, you're probably just imagining it.

As if anyone wants to imagine sleeping soundly – finally – and then waking up at 2 am or whatever-am from absolute agony. And then making a hot water bottle with rapidly boiling water which then causes 3rd degree burns (or 2nd degree, whatever). The skin on my lower back is permanently discoloured from the burns due to hot water bottles to try get at the pain in my spine. Please, with tears in my copper-blue eyes, I ask you; Explain how you *imagine* pain so bad that you fucking permanently scar and damage your skin to try get relief.

Yeah OK, pass me the anti-depressants. Let me – as the Pain Management Clinic Team so eloquently put it – "rethink" my thoughts on pain and imagine my pain is less than I think it is. Or buy shit as a distraction for the pain.

Yeah OK mate – all in my head. Just me imagining. Thanks for the reinforcement that I am a waste of space drama queen. Actually... Yeah – I mean given the fact that I believe I am a burden on those around me, and can objectively prove it to a great extent, this is a great message.

The last 5 years have all just been me imagining my little back is in pain to the extent that I am actively planning (not thinking of – planning) suicide. Told you I should depart this planet...

CORONATION DAY – Take 2

Back on the ugly, mustard-yellow chair. I hate this chair. Just the colour I mean. I'd much rather have sat on the blue chair – hold on, let me measure – 1 metre next to me. But alas, the back of that one faces the kitchen, and so when someone comes to stab me, I won't see them coming.

There are 4 blue chairs here. The aforementioned one, another one with its back to the kitchen (so same issue). Then there are 2 more blue chairs at the opposite end of the dining room from where I am. They are at first glance quite perfect – one is next to the door, back to the wall, so I can see knife-wielding attackers coming. The other is frankly perfect; in the corner, back to the wall, so quite safe.

HOWEVER, the ugly yellow chair is also in the back, in the corner, with back to the wall – BUT it is also against the 2 tiny little windows which I frequently open for fresh air. Much to the chagrin of other patients, since they want them shut. WHY THE HELL DO PEOPLE SEEM TO HATE FRESH AIR SO MUCH?

Anyway...

My wife came to visit me today.

I am so grateful that she made all the effort to drive as far as she did to come see me. It was honestly great to see her, and to go out for lunch. I miss being able to see her and enjoy simple things like a lunch with her. Just wish I were a better man, a better husband for her

It's a day I have been looking forward since she left after last Saturday's visit. But more so, since I was taken off Section on Wednesday and given free pass to wander around and come-and-go as I please. Only, *it is under condition that I remain here*, as the doctors are (and apparently will still) test some new drugs on me in the next 2 weeks.

I anticipated that the "Real World" would be a bit much, so I just asked her to bring a cheese pizza. She didn't, and suggested we go out to a nice place. Which as a suggestion was great, and I really enjoyed seeing her.

but...

HOLY MOLY! The world moves fast. What the frak! I mean have you ever noticed *just how fast the world, and people move????* After weeks of my scenery changing only as fast as I can walk, and people walking like slow zombies, being out in the Real World was a massive shock.

It was so fast
It was so loud
It was so overwhelming
It was so very much too much!

Maybe that's what's wrong with our world, you know? Maybe the problem isn't myself and the patients – maybe the problem is the pace at which society moves. By this I don't mean in some grand philosophical sense. I mean driving at 40/50/60 mph. Walking faster than I could maintain a jog. Talking loudly, being flashy and overbearing.

Hell, it's like watching primates in the zoo flash their red arses to show they are ready for mating. That's what today in the world felt like.

And the noise. Mother Mary... THE NOISE. We went to a "quaint" place called The Granary in some "Wye" town. I dropped my wife and friend off, and then went to find parking. I want you to guess how easy a task that was.

Saturday. Bank Holiday Weekend. Coronation. Touristy-town. A *Brazillion people* mulling about, walking into, across, parallel-to the roads, cars everywhere, and fuck all parking. Zip. My Spoons were spent when I got to a car park ½ a mile from the quaint restaurant, and saw it full of busses, cars, tourists and just chaos.

I drove around the little armpit of a town for a bit, left the county even at one point – all in the name of finding parking. Eventually sent my wife a text to say they should order and eat, and just get me a cheese sandwich to take away. Ironically, as I got back to the restaurant, a parking spot opened *right in front of the door*. I mean, exit the front car door, 3 steps and you're in the restaurant. WOW. The inside of the restaurant though is where I completely lost it. In an earlier (or later) chapter here, I describe how people like Dexter make me feel normal. Here's an illustration;

In the quaint restaurant were lovely slate floors.
And heavy wooden chairs.
Also aliens from the planet Zorgon 2a.

At least I think they were aliens. BECAUSE THEY COULD NOT FUCKING SIT STILL, AND KEPT LOUDLY GRINDING THE FUCKING CHAIR ON THE MOTHER FUCKING SLATE FLOOR MAKING SO MUCH CUNTING NOISE. FUCK. FUCKITY FUCK.

A nice visit with my wife for lunch, and these cockroaches making so much noise. One idiotic woman really. All I could think of was if I could cross the floor fast enough, pick up the chair, and beat the woman's skull in before anyone can realise what is happening. No, maybe grab a knife and stab her repeatedly. It would make for good sport. Plus I'd feel a lot better.

FUCK, I have become a monster!

Like I said, I am so grateful my wife came. Just wish I were able to handle Life better

FUN INTERLUDE (Saturday 6 May, 2023, 17:38 – the Common Room):

There's a patient here... If you asked me to draw Bambi, but in a human form, I'd draw this patient. She walks like deer caught in headlights. Like a scared little thing, worried about any predator that might stalk her.

Fair to say that she has had a rough few days. Night before last, she spent the night sleeping on the sofa in the Common Room.

The lounge was quite full due to just many patients being here. But I was alone at "my" table, writing this. So I invited scared Bambi to sit here, told her I'd be quiet. So she sat with a plate of food – which she didn't eat.

Whereas I literally a page or two ago wrote about cracking a woman's skull open with a wooden chair, I felt deeply sorry for this lost Bambi-like creature.

I decided to forego dinner and help her instead. I got her some ketchup, helped fetch her food and cheesecake.

But what she said stuck like a dagger in my heart;

She looked at me and said "I don't want to be here anymore". Initially, I thought she meant that she didn't want to sit with me – which is fair enough. But she started crying softly, saying that "They" (psychiatrists) are mean to her because they locked her up in here. Softly, she said "I don't want to be on this planet anymore. I just want to die in peace". Poor woman. I felt so bad. Her words stuck in my ears. In an instant, she transformed from a patient to a deeply wounded human for whom I suddenly had so much empathy – she sounded like me...

DREAMS

MAN! Dreams... Dude. Dreams... In this place. I have had some of the most awful dreams. It's been bad. Other night I dreamt that I was in some far away land, with my wife and the boys needing to come to me, but kept getting lost. To my horror in the dream, I had the cats with me who were unfed and unhappy.

The weirdest is waking up in the morning. The double-doses of sleep tablets are a godsend. It's such a cruel irony that "in the community" the sleep pills aren't freely prescribed. They make such a huge difference to me.

But waking up is wild! Most mornings, I am woken before 6 or so by the wailing and screaming (mostly from the one particular patient). It's quite harrowing. Waking up from blissful sleep with that screaming, then your mind being utterly bewildered that it doesn't know where it is. It's unreal man.

I did have ONE nice dream (2 nights ago – what, 10th of May). I dreamt my wife and I lived in Portland in the US, and I had a simple job stacking shelves at Walmart. But it was such a sunshine-filled, glorious life in the dream. Gives me some hope for the future to, for once, not have *dark* dreams...

Cat Nightmare

In one nightmare, I dreamt a fox was terrorising the house and pets. Trying to eat our old black cat. After trying to gently fight off the fox, I decided it's time to use a gun. Regrettably so, as I am a vegetarian because I feel sorry for animals. I even rescue wasps and hornets that come into the house and take them outside. So with deep reservation, I took a rifle and shot at the fox. But in the last moment, my cat leaped at the fox and tried to fight it off.

I fire several shots at the fox, but miss. So I take careful aim once more and fire. My nightmare turns into a slow-motion hellscape, as I watch the bullet twirling through the air and hit my precious silver cat in the heart. Trying to fight off the fox, I ended up killing my cat instead. With a broken heart, I put the rifle under my jaw and pulled the trigger. No ammunition left.

With horror and pain, crying hysterically, I finally woke up with a jump. Despite being just a dream, I nearly vomited when I woke up. Thankfully I had a pouch of sugar from the coffee I never drank, and poured the sugar down my throat which stopped the very real-world trauma of the nightmare, which helped me to not puke.

Some worst nightmares

In Avengers Assemble, Bruce Banner says of Loki *"His brain is a bag full of cats"*. I think that's not altogether an unfair description of me! MY brain is a bag full of cats! Proper fucked up nightmares are a staple for me currently

The following nightmare(s) are a bit out of sequence date-wise. But this felt like an appropriate place to put it. Safe to say, it's the kind of nightmares I've been having. These two specific nightmares below actually happened some time after I left the hospital. But they are generally the kind of violent, traumatising nightmare I have 4-5 out of 7 nights.

Rescuing people from Nazis;
What. The. Fuck.? HOW – please tell me how a person's mind comes up with this sort of shit? Read it, and tell me I am a "sane" human.

> This nightmare starts with me "waking up" in a prison of sorts, but with children in. Quickly I realise that I am a scientist, and I'm in Nazi Germany. Whilst I work as a doctor in the prison, I am not affiliated with the Nazis. Noticing a couple of scientists about to try an awful experiment with a child – chopping off their arms – I jump into action. I find a nail gun, and start shooting at the Nazi scientists.
>
> The nail gun, loaded with 6inch nails is quiet – and deadly. I sneak up on some guards, fire nails into the backs of their skulls. They drop dead.
>
> The dream contains various such sequences where I rescue the helpless children, making our escape every time.
>
> In the final dream sequence, I sneak into a facility and find a boy and a girl. I start sneaking them out, but they don't want to go with me. Desperately begging them to come – explaining I want

to save them – the door opens. 4 guards and a senior female nurse enter. They try stop me, but I quickly fire nails into the throats of 2 guards. One guard fires a shot at me, I fire 4 nails into him, and 2 nails into the last one's eye.

They drop dead.

Next I aim at the female nurse who is now hysterical. She's trying to shout something in a panic, trying to explain something. I fire my last nail, it hits her in the jugular, she starts bleeding.

The guard who fired his gun hit me in the leg, I cannot move. Trying to lean on a chair, I try find my feet and start loading more nails in the nail gun.

As I get to my knees, the nurse still desperately begging and pleading. With her dying breath, she says "You're safe, it's 1973. The war is over. We're trying to help…" She slumps to the floor dead.

The 2 children I came to rescue look at me in horror. I am the monster. I killed innocents in an attempt to save what I thought were victims.

My leg is bleeding.

I realise in horror the gravity of what I did.

I raise the nail gun, hold it to my head and press the trigger. I feel immense pain behind my eyes, in my sinuses. I missed. I aim higher, fire again.

I slump to the floor, my sight becoming dim. With my dying breath, I see other people rush in to help, but it's too late for me. My vision darkens and I die.

I know it's just dream – "just a dream". But I felt myself die. I felt like I died. I woke up in a panic. Realising it was just a dream, I put my earphones back in my ears and tried to listen to music to calm down.

Thank goodness I enjoy "Of Monsters and Men" and their music so much. It helped me escape to a happy mental place… until I fell asleep again.
Little did I know the next nightmare was minutes away…

Nazi Nightmare 2

After the previous nightmare, I was exhausted and fell asleep again. Only this time, I start dreaming again about a Nazi prison.

"We're all stripped naked – men and women in a small room. There's nothing sexual – we're cold and mortally afraid.

Some guards come in, and force us into a truck at gunpoint. Frightened, cold and trembling, we get into the back of an army truck.

A short ride later, we arrive at some mansion. Excitedly, we look at each other, thinking they are going to release us. Before entering, naked, we are brutally cavity searched to ensure we have no weapons hidden up our butts. The Nazi officers and violent, disrespectful – we're not even animals. They treat us like things.

They line us up in a dining hall. Seated at a long table is a group of SS officers. They point to one of the prisoners. The guards take her to the kitchen – turned out we're here because the SS officers are part of some cult who believe eating human flesh will make them 500% stronger. The one sits there and explains how we are cattle for them.

Suddenly a loud explosion rocks the house. The soldiers and officers get up and run outside. It's an American bomber attack.

The prisoners and I start running to try escape. In the confusion, I run past the stables and find a hammer. As I pick it up, a guard grabs my arm. I shake him off and continue running. Nearby there's a graveyard, I run for that. As I approach it, the guard tries to tackle me. Being stronger and faster due to the human flesh he'd been eating, he jumps too high and far. The guard falls on the floor in front of me with a thud.

Panicked, I try think of how to get away from him. But with

> instinct, I lunge at the guard, hit him on the head with the hammer. He looks enraged, and grabs my neck. With all my strength, I flip the hammer around, and hit him in the temple with the sharp claw of the hammer. The guard drops down. I hit him again in the same spot with the claw of the hammer, then the other side of his skull. Satisfied he's dead his brain spewing out of his pulverised skull, I run out of the compound to safety…"

What a fucked up set of dreams. I mean, fuck. What the fuck is going on in my head for my brain to think of shit like that??? Unbelievable. How does a person even dream of things like this?

I might have to revise my assertion that I am not mentally sick. I don't think healthy, normal people dream of such twisted, fucked up things.

Might be due to the medication I am taking. Other patients have shared their stories of how they reacted on other types of medication.

As if waking hours are not difficult enough – my brain has to screw me up like this?

It took me a good 4 hours after waking up to try recover from this shit show nightmare streak.

Again, thanks to the music by "Of Monsters and Men", I was able to sit and focus, calmed my mind and tried to shake off the very real, physical nausea and trembles from the ghastly nightmares I had.

What a horrible set of nightmares!

LAUNDRY

Onto something more banal after the nightmares…

WHAHEY!!! Friday 12 May – which happens to be a good day – I got laundry done. First time in 3 weeks. OK, maybe I've not pursued the laundry function as zealously as I could. But given that I had to wait 2 days for Morphine once, and that the one patient takes up most of the staff's time at times, laundry was low on the priority list. Especially as it's a supervised thing. You need to get one of the staff to escort you to the laundry, open your locker to get the washing powder out etc. Quite a palaver...

The laundry room is small, cramped and narrow. It reminds me of the time I lived on a British Narrowboat (aka Canal boat). Not 6ft wide, and 66ft long. But the laundry reinforces the feeling of being in a jail even more. Our lockers have our names and room numbers on – for which only a certain group of staff carry a key. Whilst we are "strongly encouraged" to do our own laundry, they also monitor us like a hawk to make sure we don't do anything to harm ourselves – I guess like eating laundry pods or drinking the detergent.

It reminds me of my first year of high school…

When I was in my first year of high school, I was so traumatised by that, that I used to drink bottles of shampoo to make myself sick so that I don't have to go to school. Sadly my parents were super strict, so despite drinking multiple bottles of shampoo, conditioner and soap over the course of the first 6 – 10 months, I was forced to go to school, sick as I was. Washing my laundry reminds me of that awful chapter in my life. Luckily, a cartoon called "Cities of Gold" was released in the later parts of my first high school year, so my mind was free to leave my body and live in the mysterious ruins of Peru and Machu Picchu. When I get back to my room now, I do the same. Watch Cities of Gold on my tablet.

Anyway, by my estimates – and if my acting is more convincing than Sarah Connor's during her review in Terminator 2 – I ought to have enough clean clothes to last until after I get home in 2 weeks. Damn, I hope I get out in 2 weeks :D

Actually, funny story; I could never understand why Sarah Connor leapt over the counter and tried to kill her psychiatrist with a *fucking pencil (*got the John Wick pencil reference?). I, in my naive little world, used to think that she should have behaved, and she might get out sooner. But now that I am rowing that boat – damn man, I can tell you, if Monday 22 May came and they decided to keep me another 6 months... Suffice to say they should keep pencils away during said review!

It's an interesting observation how people rarely fully understand (if ever) a situation, until they row that boat down that damn river. It opens your eyes.

THE THIN GLASS PANE – **Tuesday 9 May 2023**

The poem I alluded to earlier in this… document… has finally arrived in my brain:

My fingers feel the cold glass pane
First the tips
Gradually my entire hand
I marvel at the Power in the pane

First my hand resists,
Pushes against the glass in defiance
It's so thin, I could shatter it without effort
In defiance I press...

What Power it holds
To keep me in
To keep me caged
Until some revelation or enlightenment
Or until some other rescue for my soul

Daily I touch the pane
Daily it changes
Despite my pain
The pernicious Glass makes me tame

The Glass at first, an enemy to defeat
Has now become protection so discreet
The Glass at first, meant to destroy my will
Has become an invisible protection, ever still

Against a world of cruelty
A world of duality
Now my Glass pane is my saviour
Against a world incomprehensible
Against a world that flies at the speed of light
My scenery now changes at the speed of crawl
My Glass pane now protects me

Still my hands rest on that cold Glass pane
But now I'm glad, it keeps me sane
No longer do I resist
Rather glad it will persist
And tho' I'm still to die
My glass pane ensures others have no tear to cry

FAREWELL MY FRIEND

Farewell my Friend

Forty four years
A lifetime by all accounts
Through my joys and fears
The time has come to say
Farewell my Friend

A friend in need
A friend ever loyal
Ever dependable and predictable
My Friend who comforted me
A friend indeed

Before my first Year did we start
You saw me through the Sorrows
You celebrated with me through the Joys
Through times of Little you were there
Through times of Plenty, everywhere
But my Friend, sadly we now part

Thank you Coca Cola for being my Friend
Thank you Coca Cola for never judging me
Thank you Coca Cola for being a pillar of support
But now I can walk on my own, so I say goodbye
Thank you for being my Friend

Over the last month or so, I've had almost no Coke – "Red Coke", full sugar. Oi, Coke Zero and Diet are of the devil. On a normal day, I used to have 4-8 cans. Over the past month in this hospital I've probably had 6 or so – spread apart through weekly visits, as we're not allowed sugary/caffeine stuff on the ward. WITH GOOD REASON, I FOUND. It's weird. I craved it the first week. After a week of not having, it was quite a shock to the system to have some. Another week without, rarely any sugar, drinking bitter tea and water, then another Coke with a visit. WOW. That stuff is sweet. I feel like a traitor to Coke which has been such a true friend.

But the weight I've lost the past 3 weeks feels even better than drinking Coke. I'm amazed at how much weight I've lost. Even the staff say I've lost weight. But more than that, I feel I've lost weight. I feel lighter on my feet, I feel more comfortable in my body. I'm glad about that. Plus, holy moly, it will save us a lot of money per month not buying it.

But I am so very much enjoying *not having Coke*, I can hardly believe it is me writing this...

Live Long, and Prosper my Friend

UNEXPECTED VISIT

Saturday 13 May 2023. By all accounts a "hot", sunny day. It was 20-ish, not a cloud in the sky. I slept until about 1:30 – then was woken up by concerned staff that I was still sleeping. They stopped short of force-feeding me the cheese sandwich. I was awake a bit, saw the outside, and heard the joyful sound of people being outside, laughing, doing some sport, kicking a ball, practicing boxing etc.

SO I switched off the bedroom light, closed the curtains, shoved my Samsung Buds2 Pro earphones as deep into my ears as possible, and went back to sleep.

Around 5pm, one of the nicest staff members woke me up to say I had visitors. But I was whacked out, fast asleep. So I got up, sauntered to the toilet in confusion and tried to figure out who had unexpectedly come to visit.

It was my wife and oldest son. We sat outside in the sun in the front garden for a while, which was great. OK, it was over 2 hours. But it was great. Birds singing, Swallows flying... It was a super nice visit.

Probably the last visit I think. Monday after next I get out, so unlikely that they'll visit before then. So this was an absolute delightful visit.

NEXT STEPS

In the UK we have a supermarket giant called Tesco. In their Welwyn Garden City head office, you will find people with a proclivity to use the phrase "Next Steps". It's ingrained in the culture. No meeting can end without *Next Steps.* It's good actually. Focuses people's attention to actually have productive meetings where decisions are made, and people leave with some clear actions. I worked there for maybe 4 years – pretty good years on balance.

But I am sitting here in hospital tonight, a few hours from being here a week already. Nothing has changed. My back has not been fixed. My medication has not been adjusted. Aside from the fact that I had missed a date with Destiny to end my life, things have not improved. De-proved really. For a start, everyone knows what a fuckup and loser I am now.

My wife
My sons
Family
Friends
People from church

Everyone knows I am a loser who couldn't cope with a bit of pain. Where other people had carried greater burdens with grace and acceptance, I am the asshole who wanted out.

Someone from church came to visit today (name removed for privacy). He and another man from church went to Swansea to run the chapel service for 50 prisoners. I mean, just wow. What an amazing thing to do

After that, they came to visit me. Good men. Good men are hard to find you know? But they are good men. They visited with me. They encouraged me. Prayed with me. One of them said that he felt God is going to use this opportunity, now that my very foundations are broken, to build something great. I just don't see it. I feel like

Nathanael in the Bible who asked "Can anything good come out of Nazareth"? I want to ask; *"Can anything good come out of Nico?"*. Just don't see it. I feel like such a wretched failure in every aspect in life. Fuck a duck, I couldn't even commit suicide successfully.

If there were a prize for the biggest failure, I'd probably end up 2nd place.

FUN INTERLUDE (Sunday 30 April, 2023, 21:27 – the Common Room):

My room is a relatively safe place. The door has an automatic magnetic lock. Only once (when I was in a different room), did one of the patients get in because the lock wasn't working. She entered, started dancing around in my room, and promptly started rifling through my things. It was... unsettling.

Anyway, yesterday morning saw the admission of a patient called Flower (I changed her name to protect her identity, but remember her for the flowers she haphazardly drew me, which I kept).

Anyway, boy.

That was an event. She is terribly unwell, and has been shouting and throwing things around the place. For much of the night, starting again early morning. She's had to have 3-4 people within arm's length of her at all times. She tried to hug me twice, succeeding once yesterday. It was unnerving. They must have given her some sedatives, as she has been much calmer. Still unpredictable though.

She's been coming and going in the Common Room at random – handlers in tow. Just now though, she brought a huge piece of paper, with a blue marker, asked me to write my name, and drew a blue flower before signing her name with a flower.

I feel so bad for her, in wish I could help her.

Monday 1 May 2023 ... oh – "My month"...

With everything else as a prelude, today marks "My" month of recovery. But gosh, hammering away at this overly compact Bluetooth keyboard is hard work. Might need a larger one. I wonder if I'd be allowed. I call it "My" month, because in Afrikaans, May sounds the same as the word "My" – denoting ownership. My sister used to confuse the two, and tell our parents things that happen in "her month" – May. So in honour of that, I call it "My month" – but also because May offers me a chance to heal…

Patients in the Mental Health hospital have a litany of things they're not allowed to have – for safety's sake. Though, I maintain I do not have a mental health condition. And ending my life certainly does not involve cables. It's the last thing I'd ever do for myself, it would be with love, care and mercy. Anyway, lots of things are on the restricted list and some patients might have other things that are restricted. But a bigger keyboard might be nice.

This morning we did pottery. I've never done pottery before. It's not the whole spinny-wheel thing. It's actually quite calm and soothing (2 points if you can guess why they offer pottery...). It's so very soothing. Just handling the clay, getting to know it, and finding out what shape it wants to take, is so immensely soothing.

A month ago when I was here voluntarily, I made the half DNA helix symbol from the TV show Heroes. It's actually a Japanese Kanji that means "Godsend";
Anyway, it came out great.

It's the only tattoo I have. A number of years ago – actually just over a decade now – I got this as a tattoo. It resulted from a period of time when work was *immensely* tough going. We lived maybe 40 miles north of London, and I had to commute into London for work. Only, due to the place this company was, going by train or tube was not an option. Nor was the bus.

So I had to drive this dog-ugly Peugeot van, a 1997 Peugeot Expert. My wife bought it because she was going to do childminding, and I was going to drive my glorious 330i, straight six, automatic BMW to London. But she hated the van, and decided against childminding, so I was stuck with that ugly van. Manual gearbox, propensity to overheat, a fix for which was driving with the heating on full. This was not a problem in winter, but man, summers were hell!

Anyway, during that time, I had a baptism of fire at work. It was insanity. But I kept drawing that Godsend sign on my left wrist as a reminder for myself that I can push through the tough spots in life. I always thought I could push, I could with sheer willpower, overcome every hardship and obstacle life throws at me. Apparently not – I mean here I am in a mental hospital because I am so weak.

Maybe I should have the tattoo removed? I hate hypocrisy and well, having that tattoo is now a lie, is it not? I'm not that strong after all. Quite the opposite. Just some weak fuck

OH MY WWORDDDD!!!!!!!!!!!!!!

I JUST RAN out of the Common Room. Bloody hell, a person can only take so much. One of the patients keeps moaning and laughing/crying in an unnaturally loud voice. She was out for the weekend – I forgot how loud she is. Plus, I only eat 2x cheese sandwiches in a day, and despite making a grand lunch for everyone, they forgot to make my cheese sandwich. Luckily I'm able to, and often do, go days without eating. So fuck eating. I am actually relieved.

The worst is having misophonia. Misophonia is a disorder in which certain sounds trigger an emotional or psychological response so strong, that most people consider unreasonable in the circumstance. The sound of chewing fucking apples, eating, slurping and related food noises – clanging plates and cutlery... few people realise how close they've come to death at my hands. The number of times I've wanted to dig a teaspoon into someone's skull and dig their brains out, or drown them in that bowl of soup for being so ... so... SO

FUCKING LOUD AND IRRITATING AND DISGUSTING WHILST THEY EAT LIKE A FAT SWINE.

Oh – *random* thought; Do most people have this reaction? If not, maybe it's evidence that I do need to be in a mental hospital. After all, if wanting to drill a blunt teaspoon into someone's skull whilst you eat is not normal – if anyone ever reads this, let me know if this describes you, or if it is just me who is this insane.

I'm back in the sanctuary of my room. I couldn't stand all the food noises, and that woman weeping and moaning. Unfortunately, she's finished eating now, and in the outdoor quad.

I will allow you, dear reader, 47 guesses if my room faces into the slap bang centre of the quad, as well as being a point at which sound converges. I've dug my Samsung Earbuds so deeply into my ears, the rubber tips came off and are now stuck in my ears. But I just need some relief from the noise. Going to pull my blanket and pillows over my head for a bit...

A GOOD DAY - Friday 12 May 2023

Ha! I didn't see that coming, did I? Having an actual good day. It's 14:37 as I write this from my mustard-yellow chair, and *not once did I think of suicide today*! Not once. WOW. It's been a few moons since I had a day like this...

One of the patients was well enough to go home today. He thanked me for being a "lifesaver". What did I do to deserve this? Nothing really. I gave him access to my super-fast, unlimited EE WiFi hotspot, and chatted some Star Trek with him. Turned out that he was profoundly grateful about the WiFi hotspot – indeed being very anxious about it when the hospital's WiFi didn't work for him.

I went with to the shop this morning. The lovely activities coordinator invited me to the shop on Tuesday. I had no interest in going, but I wanted salted peanuts, and trusted nobody else to get me proper peanuts. I mean if it's not KP Nuts, are they even worth eating? Anyway, that's what I was after, so I went with. Absolutely manky-smelling Ford Kuga (NHS car). But it felt good to get out – and get out slowly. I think I was writing about the disastrous visit with my wife and friend, where I lost my mind because life was going so fast at 60mph. But the shop run of today and Tuesday hardly reached 30mph. Also, I was not driving. It was a nice stress-relief.

"Fun" – rather tragic really – Interlude

As stated, we went to the shop today. One of the female patients came with. If you've ever watched the movie K-Pax, she's like the one with the jewellery in that movie.

I noticed she had 2 "Caterpillar" party cakes. Generic SPAR version

She was counting out the small change from her wallet over the counter, repeatedly apologising for taking so long. But she told the cashier it was her birthday the next day, hence the cakes. For the other patients, you see?

I feel so sorry for her. She always tries to do her hair in pony tails etc, but she always ends up looking a little dishevelled.

She enjoys meal times tremendously, and always thanks the staff most gratefully, saying "It was Beautiful, BEAUTIFUL, absolutely BeaUtiful!". Seems like the general living environment in this hospital is orders of magnitude better than what she has at home. I wonder for how many people that is true? That their lives behind this Glass Pane are so much better than anything they can achieve at home. Life is cruel...

I bought her a box of Ferrero Rocher and put it in a nice gift bag. Didn't cost much. And really, I only did it because I felt so sorry for her being here on her birthday.

However, I was unprepared for the immense gratitude this small token would elicit. As slow as I am with my aching back, I deftly managed to dodge a hug, and just awkwardly said she's welcome.

She started crying.

I was not prepared for such a tiny – on balance pretty much worthless – token to be so gratefully received. People here have little, and to those who have so little, doing even something very little for them is met with the greatest gratitude. It's funny how

> when you've lost pretty much everything in life – including your dignity – things that would have been trivial previously are now so wonderful.
>
> *These poor souls*

Things have calmed down in the ward overall.

The patient I described as the "Banshee" – the one who drew me the flower – caused most of the ruckus. She arrived about 3 days or so after I did, has been taking at least 40% of the staff's time. It's a rough estimate, but if you think of the total staff count, one patient taking at least 40% of their time is a lot!

She's now been put – sadly, I might add – in solitary confinement. But it is better for everyone else.

She caused a lot of disruption, without apparently being aware of her actions. She also had exclusive use of the Library, a place I'd normally go to for solitude, so it's been rough for me. Plus 2 other very vocal, "physically engaging" patients have been discharged. The ward has become quite peaceful over the past 2 days. IF you can ignore the violent banging on the door, and screams of the aforementioned patient. Nights have been difficult, even with double sleep pills.

Last night even was fairly rough. I had lots of pain, only 5ml of Morphine on occasion – not even when I ask, as the staff are too busy running around putting out proverbial fires that rowdy patients start.

But today has been a fairly good day.

And have I said how amazing my lavender purple Samsung Galaxy Buds2 Pro are?? WOW. What a difference. They fit well, don't fall out all the time, shield me from the noise and produce amazing music. I LOVE my earphones!

I'll park Friday there for now – a nice positive note, which is something I've not had or felt for a while.

(Side note; Monday 15 May – Friday was to be the last positive day for a while. I ended up sleeping from about an hour after I wrote this until 3pm on Monday. I feel so down and useless and depressed. Just didn't see much point in getting up, or eating or whatever all weekend. I'm up now because even in my depressed state, I realise I had to go shower at some point. Which I've now done, so back to bed. I just wish my pointless existence would end)

MONDAY 15 May

It's a week until I go home. A bit traumatising – the reality of the cold, heartless, uncaring world is just outside this *thin glass pane*. Part of me so desperately wants to go home. Another part of me almost wishes I'd never be discharged... I am so fearful of how to re-adjust to the outside world, which has not spent 4+ weeks in a mental hospital. In fact, by my estimate, all-in, I've now spent around 20% of my entire year thus far to now in a damn mental hospital.

Google keeps sending me memories of "This day in history". It's so jarring, and not for a moment would I have thought a year hence, I'd be in a mental hospital. Can you imagine getting those reminders in May 2024? The ugly mustard yellow chair...

There is also the question of use or belonging. My family is getting by pretty well in my absence. Nice revision of the old "Trolley" problem where you must choose to switch a train track to either hit one person, or many. I'm that one person – from my interactions with family, the train can gladly run right over me and all would be OK. In fact, with the month's space they've had from me, it's all the much easier for them if the train did run over me – their sadness, irritably and trouble with having me at home will be instantly alleviated. Not having the stench of my presence around.

ALSO

I am out of medicine.

FUCK!

The only meds that truly works for me. I'm told by the hospital that it wasn't on some list, but they have ordered some. Next few days are in for some chop. Not great.

Parsimonious

Given freely to lesser sires
Begrudgingly chucked at the Greatest
Lavishing upon them with joy
Parsimoniously dripped for the Greatest

Engagement with vigour and exuberance
Yet now as exciting as a beached whale
They paid not for the sins of others
Unlike the Greatest who pays for all sins

But you're the Greatest!
You were Chosen!
You are Special!

Naught but words
For actions show it not
For what was given freely to lessers
Is meagrely age begrudgingly counted for you

NEW KEYBOARD!! – 15 May 2023

Post normally arrives around 16:30 in the hospital. That's just because the post room – whom I am certain stole my first set of Galaxy Pro2 buds – bring all the day's parcels around that time.

I've been waiting for my new keyboard since what, Thursday or so. One of the staff brought it to me at 22:30 only – lost in the *ever busy* staff office.

But no matter. It is here. AND IT WORKS! Artek brand, same as the previous 4 year old, and much travelled one. This one is a delight! AN ABSOLUTE DELIGHT.

I've pretty much decided to stop adding to this *Collection of words and pages*, as it's mostly self-important, self aggrandising, boring, predictable horse-shit.

But I am loving the tactile sensation of this wonderful new keyboard, so I am writing a bit of whatever. I love how this keyboard feels though.

The tactile sensation of pressing the buttons feels... comforting in a way. Soothing. I'll add some more words, just so I can feel the lovely keyboard under my fingertips.

Sleeping lions

MAYDAY! MAYDAY!
The captain panicked for help,
As the battleship slipped beneath the waves

HELP! HELP!
Cried the helpless the baboon
Carried off in lion's mouth

MERCY! MERCY!
Screamed the victim
Receiving Wrath's violence

Pity the battleship fired the first shot
Pity the monkey poked the sleeping lion
Pity the victim was the first to strike

So often we side with the poor victims
So often we scold the apparent aggressors
Yet rarely we realise they were victims first

Minding their own business.
Peacefully sleeping.
Innocently living.

Pity then the victims not
Their disaster their own making
Retribution well-deserved

ON: THE SPEED OF LIGHT

I never realised how much of our lives are impacted by the speed of light. It's not just some cosmic thing "out there".

Take the Periodic Table of Elements for example. A set of basic visualisations on the number of elements we currently know of. 118 in fact, as of May 2023.

Now, Science Fiction often talks about weird, fanciful materials with odd names like "Unobtanium" (from Avatar). But have you ever stopped to think how the speed of light limits the kinds of material that can exist?

Simply put, an atom consists of a neutron, around which electrons orbit.

But the electrons can only orbit the neutron up to the speed of light.

That places an upper limit to the speed at which they can orbit, and at these higher speeds, the particles might exist in higher energy states. At these higher energy rates, particles might exist that we do not yet know about. However, the faster an electron spins around the neutron, the shorter-lived the atom is, so you might have very high state particles that very rapidly decay.

So they could exist but exist for such a short period of time that they decay so fast, we would struggle to measure them in everyday life.

Anyway, just a random thought

THE PODCAST – 16 May 2023

In the Lord of the Rings books – I think Return of the King – JRR Tolkien wrote about the *"Deep breath before the plunge" (maybe it was just the movie)*. At any rate, it's a discussion about fear and death and what is about to come. The inevitability of an event that will forever change the course of Life.

2-ish weeks ago, I recorded a Podcast with someone I worked with 12 years ago. I was hesitant at first. I never agree to these things, particularly because I neither see myself as a wise/worthy enough a human, nor a good enough leader to talk on podcasts. But I agreed to talk to this gentleman, particularly as he wanted to discuss Leadership and vulnerability. And you know – being under Section in hospital because you tried to commit suicide is pretty vulnerable.

Anyway. We spoke. An hour – just short of. Broadly covering where I was born, grew up, the exciting story about me dropping Mathematics in my 1st year of High School, then trying to catch up with 5 years' worth of Trigonometry, Algebra and Geometry in my last 6 months of High School.

But I also spoke at some length about my being Sectioned, and being here in hospital. Mostly my self-important horse shit about trying to help people. FffuuuccckkkK, I am so full of shit. Pretending I can help others.

Anyway, the podcast is being released tomorrow 17 May, as part of Mental Health Week.

If Life were a video game, this is the part I'd have hit the SAVE button hard, because this can go terribly wrong. For a start, once that video is out – once you fire that bullet, you cannot get it back in the gun. It's out. It might well end my career.

I mean, who wants to employ a suicidal maniac, locked up in a mental hospital???

But like other people said, if someone doesn't want to employ me on those grounds, is that even someone you want to work for/with? Probably not...

So here's the deep breath before the plunge. The next 12 hours might ruin me, or open a set of new doors I cannot imagine.

Eternally optimistic dick on a donkey

HACKSAW RIDGE

The podcast reminded me of Hacksaw Ridge, so I watched it again.

I ~~never~~ rarely watch war stories. Rather; I rarely watch movies that deal with WW1 or WW2. I've read enough history and studied enough of history to know some of the awful things that happened in those wars. Atrocities committed by the "Axis" powers, as well as the Allied Nations. If you don't believe in Evil, give me a few minutes with a history book. Guarantee you'll probably puke your guts out around the same time you start to realise Evil is a thing.

Anyway, Hacksaw Ridge is different to other war movies. Based on the true story of an absolute legend of a man called Desmond Doss. You probably – I certainly – cannot watch that movie without shedding a tear. The bravery and courage in the face of such barbarity... WOW

Anyway, Desmond Doss (in Real Life) said that when he was on the Ridge, alone, in the dark, covered with blood and mud, prayed "*Lord, just One More*". The courage and strength to save *just one more person*. Then after that, "Lord, Just One More". Doss saved around 75 people during one night when the Americans tried to take a beach in Japan.

That's been my motto of late – "Just One More". In terms of helping people in everyday life, on LinkedIn, or here in hospital. Just One More. Not that I was even thinking of Desmond Doss, nor do my pitiful deeds in total add up to a minute of Desmond Doss on the Ridge.

But my efforts are sincere. I gave a patient my wireless solar charger because she was anxious about charging her phone in the laundry area (where we're supposed to charge them). I gave a few other patients my personal WiFi hotspot access, because the hospital's one is awful. The hospital's IT people don't seem to realise that the entire place is a Faraday Cage, which absorbs WiFi signal – *and that's why the pretty good WiFi is so bad!* I've hung my one phone on the curtain rail, so it gets uninterrupted outside signal at around 100Mbps, and then that bounces around inside the hospital for myself and other patients to share. EE was kind enough to give me an entire month of unlimited fast hotspot, just because I am *in this place*. THANK YOU EE! You have no idea how much that means to us!

At some point this weekend, the hospital messed up the dinner food order for us all.

I've not been eating much, so had a few cheese sandwiches still wrapped up in the fridge. On Saturday night they were understaffed, so got some agency workers in to cover the NHS shifts.

A few of the patients were already gathering at the sliding hatch where they dispense the food from 20-30 minutes before 22:00. But since it was *agency* staff, they took longer, and by 22:45 there was a near-riot by people who were so hungry, angry and agitated (Hangry my family calls it). But to top it all off, the catering company sent too few sandwiches. So the hangry patients were getting quite upset. Luckily I had the leftover sandwiches, and despite me actually being hungry for once, I told the staff to give it to these other patients instead, and went to bed.

Hardly noble or noteworthy. I just mention it ... – I guess as part of my eternal struggle to justify being alive?

You know, if I do more for others than myself – giving more than I take, if I sacrifice for the good of others, it means I am allowed to live a week more. It's like those early Nintendo games where you had to race around a track with the clock running down. But if you complete a lap, you get 20 seconds more. That kind of thing, concept rather, is in my head, trying to justify why I should be on this planet for any more time – trying to do good by others. If I give the patients my uneaten cheese sandwiches, I would therefore be allowed to live for 2 hours extra.

Anyway – my own trivial little actions. Most things I do for others, I don't/didn't/will never write about, because that's not why you do things for others. You do it for their sake, to help them, not glory. I only wrote it down here to remember I did something for others, and are therefore allowed by my own fucked up value system, to breathe a bit more. Not like anyone will read this shit.

Back to Hacksaw Ridge; I watched it tonight, at the utter depths of my emotional state, wondering if that's a good enough excuse to keep existing? Maybe through the course of my wretched life, I am able to help Just One More person. Then after, Just One More. *I wonder if I should get a tattoo of that on my arm...*

So tonight I am conflicted. I so badly want to end my life. But if I can help Just One More human, damn, why not? But is that really reason enough to justify my own existence? Surely others are there to help? That's what annoys me about myself, this self-inflated sense of purpose through service and sacrifice. There are *more than enough* people out there who serve and sacrifice for others, you fucking idiotic dick on a donkey!

Why should I matter???

THE JOB INTERVIEW... (also 16 May 2023)

16 May 2023 has turned out to be a pretty big day. I feel absolutely dismal, spent most of my day in bed, earphones on, curtains drawn, lights off and refusing to even eat.

At 15:44 I got a call from the recruitment agency about the next stage in the job interview. I was ready to die tonight. But I promised I'd see this job thing through.

They've decided to scrap the Technical Test part of the interview, seeing as they want a unicorn who can come in and solve problems. Problems they don't know exist, cannot predict will exist or how to approach. Or test. So they scrapped the tests.

Instead, I have a 1 hour interview with a couple of senior people on Thursday at 2pm. So that is the anvil on which the hammer will fall. Thursday 2pm – that will determine the course of my life.

Fail, I am ready to die here in this hospital. I am ready and thoroughly prepared.

Pass, well, I guess I see where the rabbit hole goes?

DEATH'S HOUR

The Hour most people dread
An hour filled with mystery
An hour's end filled with dread

Few know the time
Few know the hour
The hour that Death's hammer will strike the anvil

But I know mine
I know the trigger
I know the feeling
I know the hour when I'll resign

Leave Life's misery
Leave Life's struggle and madness
And gift those around me my absence

An hour I am well prepared for
An hour that I am ready for
I just need the trigger
And the last laugh will be mine to snigger

CHRISTOPHE'S GIFT

It's been a heavy night. Fighting with Death, trying to avoid looking for the tiniest glimmer of hope. I've put in so much effort and pain into deciding to end my life, even a glimmer of hope is rather unwelcome. Trust me, deciding to end your life is no easy thing! People might "feel suicidal", but I don't think many truly live through the gravity of that set of decisions.

And yet, after watching Hacksaw Ridge last night, I am confronted with the profound truth that my life is not over quite yet. And until it ends, there is a chance that I can help *Just One More* person in life.

It's not much, I'll grant.

My help that is. But even on a fierce dark ocean, in the midst of a terrible storm, a basic life ring is of utmost value to the person drowning. So, maybe that is *my purpose* from now on. To throw life rings to those who feel like they're drowning, so that they can stay afloat until real rescue arrives.

A life ring.

A plain, simple orange life ring with some reflective strips. Most are unused for their entire life – but if they save *Just One Life*, then their entire purpose is complete.

I've accepted in Life that I will never be the big hero guy. Rather just the fat dick on a donkey. But even the dick on the donkey can throw a life ring into the sea to help someone. And though it is nothing grand, and great and wow – *to one person, it might make a difference*...

Around noon-thirty somewhere, a member of the nursing staff walked up to me with an Amazon parcel. They have to watch you open parcels (for obvious reasons). I hadn't ordered anything, but I opened it up with great care – to reveal a silver-wrapped gift inside.

It shone like Mithril in the sun. I took a photo of

The Mithril gave way to an exquisite Notebook – the cover instantly excited me as it was a depiction of Bilbo Baggins, escaping from the Elves on a barrel, with the rest of the dwarves inside the barrels.

Before I even looked inside the notebook, I told the nurse with tearful eyes *"This is a gift from a great man. Many people think they are friends, even good friends to people. But the man who sent me this, is a man of true courage. A man who understands that sometimes friends need to say tough things to friends they love and care for."* I then looked at the nurse and said *"He is the most courageous man I know"*.

I opened it, and inside he wrote the famous quote by Gandalf "All we have to do decide, is what to do with the time that is given to us".

Signed simply ChL – such an elegant signature from a man greater than most alive. Thank you my friend

A rather profound confirmation of my realisation last night that all I need to do, is help Just One More human on their journey in life...

THE ANVIL HAS BEEN STRUCK
The final hammer has struck the final anvil
The final die is cast,
There now is no turning back
Things are now in motion
They're for others to decide – for good or evil

The Job Interview is done
Death stands in the corner of my room
His scythe, a comforting sign of doom
The hooded, dark-cloaked figure waits in patience
My blood runs cold as his breath fills the room

Yet, I am ready for this doom
For the last hammer to at long last destroy the last anvil
In peace though, I am biding my time
Waiting for the inevitable blow
Seven days to wait – an eternity

But I am ready, I am prepared
Frankly I am excited
For the pain to end
For my worthlessness to end
For my wretched, unmemorable life to be spent.

As soon as I get the word "No"
I'll proceed like the Emperor in Star Wars;
Order 66 will commence
And I'll be out of here

The funniest is that I've had 2 room searches. Random searches they go through your stuff at random. But I was remarkably clever with the planning and hiding of my *final solution*. It's so obvious really, anyone with eyes could spot it. But I think it is because it's so obviously hidden that nobody realises it.

I win ☺

2024: Please allow me the dignity of denying what I said here

THE ANOREXIA TABLE (Friday 19 May 2023, 17:30)

Well, isn't this an interesting chapter for the *dick on the donkey*...?

Today I got into trouble today! I mean for real. Hate being in trouble

A nurse came and sat *really* close to me in an effort to truly get her point across. She stared me dead in the eyes, her face less than 6 inches from mine.

It was a conversation I have been dreading. **I. MUST. EAT.**

FUCK.

Since I got here (and the week and change in my first stint), I have eaten nothing but cheese sandwiches twice a day at most, with some bitter tea. Just 2 slices of bread with some cheese (rarely do they put butter on).

Breakfast and I don't go well together ever, so that's nothing new. But this damn hospital keeps trying to make us eat.

And I've not had access to, what is effectively unlimited "Red Coke" at home. I've been drinking mainly water, with sugar-free squash in. Suffice to say I've lost a fair amount of weight. 7kg or so in the last 4 weeks.

Oh, funny story – I've also lost 2cm – 3cm in height, due to my back. If anyone was wondering if I truly had back issues, there's your proof. I've become shorter!

Back to the hospital and *food*.

For someone with autism, it's actually a comfortable rhythm in hospital. Soothing. But paradoxically, I also do not want to be held by the schedule. I like knowing it exists. But I do not want to be subjected to it.

Every 2 hours they open the food hatch (dunno what they really call it). But it seems to me more like a feeding trough for animals on a farm than anything else.

Every 2 hours, they hand out sandwiches, biscuits and warm drinks. That's aside from lunch and dinner which are grand occasions. Grander still are Sunday lunches. You'd be hard-pressed to find better eating at most restaurants, even compared to mid-week meals here. Cake or some snazzy dessert every day as well.

But it has not escaped the hospital staff's keen sense of observation, nor their *prodigious* note-taking, that I have been refusing to eat. It started with me just asking them to leave my sandwiches in the fridge "for later", which I purposely intend on not eating. Then it progressed to me not even filling in the menu every day – just pretending that I did it. So no food gets made for me, which is a convenient excuse to not eat. But even this has not pleased the staff.

Fast-forward to today, and the nurse came to sit right in front of me, "*ask-ordering*" me to eat at least the lunch sandwich.

One thing I can tell you, dear reader, is that you never want to get into this kind of position in a facility like this.

Granted I've not often been in such a facility, but assuming a reasonably homogenous NHS training setup, and reasonably similar kind of person who does this job, I assume that most Mental Health Facilities/Hospitals are like this.

You know the phrase "Now the gloves come off"? Well – DREAD THE MOMENT ONE OF THE STAFF MEMBERS SAY "RighT" – with a rather explosive accent on the T. Because what follows "RighT", is *that the gloves come on.*

Mate, once the gloves come on, you're up a creek without a paddle. If you ever are in such a situation, you only have yourself to blame. I've noticed the "RighT" situation a few times. The calm, friendly NHS staff can suddenly become quite ... "persuasive".

Anyway, I realised today that the nurse was giving me an exit off the highway that went to destination "RighT". So I ate the damn sandwich. Not the banana though.

So now I am made to sit at the "Anorexia Table". And please, I mean no disrespect by saying this. In fact;

One of the ladies is a bit older than me, reminds me a lot of my mom.

Shorter than me, small frame, but you can see a strong, proud woman in her – it's just like all of us here, Life has just kicked her in the teeth once too many. She often makes use of my "Quiet Space" outside of feeding times. Even if it's just a brief 3 minute sit-down. But rarely speaks. She just sits in the safety of the space I made, comforted that she's able to sit at a table with another human without having to engage.

I've learned that my Quiet Space is a nice anchor for people – they can come and go, and I'm here whenever they're round.
How tragic is that though? That the dick on the donkey's "Quiet Space" is something people value. How sad their lives must be that *my presence* is something they value!

> INTERLUDE – It's now exactly 34 minutes since I went to the office to ask for morphine and they said "5 minutes"...

Anyway, the other lady at the Anorexia Table is only 18.

As young as my youngest son – at time of writing. She's remarkably intelligent. Frankly, other than my 2 boys, she has the greatest amount of intellect and wide-ranging interests that I've ever seen in someone so young.

She also often comes to sit in my Quiet Space. Sometimes we just stare into our bitter tea, other times we chat. I make a point of not talking a lot – I am here for others to talk to/at, not for me to assault with what I consider interesting trivia.

Anyway, it makes me sad to see her at the "Anorexia Table". The other lady is around 66 I think. But at 18?! And she's just *here*. Arrived a week ago, no- absolutely zero talk of leaving. They've just put her here. I feel for her. 18 year olds shouldn't be in hospitals like this! They should be out experiencing Life, you know?

What a cruel fucker Life is.

I mean, on balance she has it "easy" if you think of children, very young children who have terminal diseases. I guess it's just that she's 18 and I know how much my youngest son is enjoying driving around Wales in his Mazda MX5, whilst she's stuck here. At least she knows about things like History, Languages, Physics etc, so we have some more engaging conversations than what is the norm here.

Still, it's sad that a highlight of her and the other lady's day is to sit with the dick on a donkey at a table.

Other patients also make frequent use of the Quiet Space. Most are just to quietly sit and reflect.

The men are again, most interestingly, pretty quiet. Say a few words, then drift off, with their eyes drenched in pain before they realise where they are and say some more words. Three men in particular have been very sad to sit with. I mean their circumstances. Unlike the cruel, fast outside world, we're all fairly open with our troubles in this place. Well, the women are less likely to state *why* are here. Maybe they just don't feel comfortable sharing with a man?

But the men often open up in the Quiet Space. One tries to hide his pain by being buff and doing weights and exercise. He made himself a cool T-Shirt that reads on the front; "Don't just wear a T-Shirt that says you workout." Then on the back; "Build a body that shows you do".

He often comes, sits down, says 7 or 18 words, jumps up to go *vape* outside, then back to say a few more words. He wears sunglasses often. At least with other staff and patients he rarely takes them off. But he removes them almost without fail when he sits by me. It's not always polite, I think, to look people in the eye. People don't like you looking into their souls. But I've looked him in the eye a few times, my mouth saying some or other as a distraction while I look into his eyes. Sitting here on the ugly mustard-yellow chair, I think of him and I come close to tears. There's a deeply scarred, badly wounded soul behind those eyes.

The other guy, man, I feel for him also. About my age judging by the greying of his beard. Knows a lot about Star Trek – but not enough to know things like what a Sarium Krellide Power cell is (They are the "batteries" in Star Trek Next Generation that they use from shuttles to phasers).

Anyway, Poor guy. He has a young child – a few months old. He's trying to read a book about Fatherhood, but clearly struggles with attention. I suggested Audible to him today before he went home on weekend leave.

His eyes often wander off into the distance. Talk to him and he'd say something or hear a word that triggers some buried trauma and his mouth just mumbles as his brain disengages to save him the pain. He'd stare out the window, or even just the wall. Pain etched into every crease and fold in his skin, his eyes almost seem to darken. Sometimes, an unwelcome tear escapes, and more frequently than he'd probably like, the tear runs and is followed by others, like a river in the desert down his cheek.

Then, by some unknown mechanism, his attention returns to the present, often embarrassed by his mental slip up.

Each of these patients – and many others, I have studied them all very carefully. Some like me "talking" with my hands – using gestures to clarify anything I say. Others need me to just keep my arms folded, and speaking with a gentle voice so as to not startle them, or hurt them by accidentally speaking a few decibels too loud.

Others seem to prefer a much slower pace of talking, or indeed a much faster one. One guy told me I talk too slowly!

It is an irony – a damn tragic one – that I, a person who understands humans the least, would study them, get to know them and accommodate them in every word, gesture and inflection of my voice. These people need a Great Man. They need someone who "gets" them, who can meet them where they're at, and just make them feel better by the fact that they're in his presence.

Instead, they're stuck with a dick on a donkey. It aggravates me so much. I wish I would stop doing this – trying to help people when I am patently incapable of helping myself!

A SMALL MEASURE OF PEACE – Friday 19 May 23:22

I am still sitting in the Day Room/Common Room, 2 hours after I asked for the Morphine which never came.

As I am sitting here, waiting, reflecting, I suddenly had a realisation that drove me to literal tears;

Everyone is just trying to find a small measure of peace.

Tears stream down my face as I think of my fellow patients. An avalanche of water pours from my eyes onto my keyboard, phone and table.

One patient whom I was particularly cruel to once, comes to mind. She has been going around the hospital and quad outside my room doing this moaning /groaning /weeping kind of thing. I recall her being outside really early (before 7am) one morning making that sound. Frustrated and exhausted from a night of people screaming, I shouted "SHUT THE FUCK UP" She didn't hear me. But the fact is that I did that, I know I did it.

Tonight, per sheer happenstance, I overheard a nurse explaining to another nurse that this lady had some trauma (I didn't hear what), and that she is in fact "singing" to herself to calm herself.

That poor woman!

So broken. So traumatised. Trying to find a small measure of peace, and here I am shouting at her to shut the fuck up.

I am simultaneously overcome with the realisation of just what a horrid, monster of a human I am, as well as a profound sense of tragic sadness for her. What horrors befell that poor woman that brought her here? Hardly any teeth left, struggling to speak, she sings to herself to try calm herself against the monsters that haunt her in her mind.

It's a good confirmation for me why I need to end my life. Monsters like me don't deserve Life!

That I could have been so cruel to someone. Someone who is so broken she hardly ever realises where she is. But takes the time to shower every day as if driven by some internal mechanical instinct, she puts pretty beads and clips in her hair for reasons unknown. Unknown to us, and probably unknown to her as well. I am beset by a tremendously heavy burden for these poor people I share a space with. I wish I could have helped. I wish anyone could help.

What has gone wrong with the world – so incredibly wrong, that humans can be so broken? How can a sentient being get so utterly broken? How is our society so very technologically advanced, building Artificial Intelligence, but that even now is *incapable* of healing mental health issues.

Yet we – I as one of them – so callously and with nary an effort hurt, and scar and break others. It seems to me that it would have been better if we could all just realise that *we all are just seeking a small measure of peace.*

If I make it out of this hospital – and I caveat that "If" heavily, I would like to take more time to look people in the eye, to truly see them and to do less harm to others.

It's so easy to harm.

The Mortal wound

The Mortal wound
So callously inflicted
With so little effort inflicted
It cuts to their heart
It cuts to their core
Yet, so callously do we inflict that wound

I look around and see people
They each irritate and annoy
They grate and irritate
For each I have a personalised insult!
They are all so feeble!
Then from nowhere an unstoppable Wave;
It washes from my eyes the mud and clay of judgement
as I look around I see people,
So hopelessly hurt and broken
So desperately a *small measure of peace they crave*

The power of the Wave is immense
It rolls me, and tumbles me
It washes over me, and through me
And suddenly I see without pretence;

Hurt people
Broken people
Defeated people
Their Scars run deep,
like Eternity's footprints in granite

The Wave, now within me;
It washes through my eyes
The tears flow like an unstoppable flood
As I see my fellow patients with new eyes

Oh Lord, if I make it out alive;

Please grant me the heart
To treat people with more care
To do less damage, and do more good
And maybe for just one soul,
Help them find *a small measure of peace*

SATURDAY VISIT (20 May 2023)

My wife and a friend came to visit today. A most glorious, Welsh summer day, literally not a cloud in sight and I have photographic evidence to prove it!

They brought medium Domino's Pizza, and we just sat here in the sun eating pizza. If not for the red armband room "key" on my wrist, it would easily have been just like any fun, enjoyable day out. From sitting on the rustic old benches, to the sunshine, birdsong and laughter to some nice food.

I did almost make our friend die from shock and horror and laughter when I casually mentioned "Surprise Euthanasia" – a concept I've been toying with. It was clear that "Surprise Euthanasia" was not in either my wife, nor friend's daily vocabulary. But I'll write about that some other time...

It was so good to just *be*. Just sit there in the sun. Watch people come and go, patients smile under the warming sun and just enjoying being alive. As if, for a million light-years the Earth is the only planet on which creatures sit under their warming primary star, blissfully unaware of the Universe at large.

Devoid of a struggle to find meaning or purpose, just living in the moment, experiencing joy in the smallest moments. Gentle rays of sunshine which travelled through 93 million miles of cold, dead space – only to gently caress every skin exposed.

MY WORD! What an exquisite planet. In all the known universe, the only planet we presently know of that can sustain complex life. The only planet where sentience thrives. Quite possibly the only place where beauty and meaning exists in a vast, unfathomable cosmos.

What a beautiful day

ANGELS IN BLUE AND GREEN

I've been fairly critical of the NHS in these pages. And for good reason, I think. For years, I have begged and pleaded for help, but my pleas were ignored and shut up with another half litre bottle of Morphine.

HOWEVER, I have also in the course of the last few years met NHS staff who were absolutely not human. I mean that in a good way. I'm a bit tired, so my vocabulary is as good as whatever. Superhuman? Yeah, ok, let's use that word. Superhuman.

I asked the nurse who made me sit at the "Anorexia Table" to come sit with me while I had tea. Let's call her ... "Amber" (not her real name). Not her real name, but my Synaesthesia turns her into Amber that shines gold in the sunlight.

I caught a glimpse of Amber rapidly exiting the building earlier, through the Common Room door – did not seem like "protocol". As she briefly glimpsed up to swipe her ID card to unlock the door, I thought I caught a tear in her eyes.

So like a trapdoor spider, I timed my bitter tea request for the very last moment and asked Amber to sit with me. The chap behind the counter momentarily being annoyed that I waited until the last minute to ask for tea, only to remember I don't normally give them grief, so he acquiesced to the request. He promptly closed the shutter and the other patients dispersed, leaving Amber and myself alone in the Common Room. Not an unusual sight, and plain in the open, so nobody would think it strange.

With little else to give, I offered Amber a custard cream (which I heard her once tell someone she loves). With purpose, I stared into my bitter tea and asked Amber if she's OK.

Silence.

I decided to press; "You brighten up the days in this place like amber glowing in the sun. Earlier I saw you leave the building, visibly upset. Are you OK?"

I glanced up. She was staring at the table, tears running down her cheek. I looked back at my tea. I waited.

Amber shifted in her chair. "It's nothing, just a misunderstanding", she offered.

I pressed my lips, and purposely slowly raised my head to meet her eyes. Slowly I spoke; "It seemed like more than nothing. Someone clearly upset you. You have been so kind and gracious to everyone you meet, even when it seemed that nobody was watching you, you go the extra mile for people, always with a smile if you meet someone's eyes. You are a rare gem in a cold, heartless world Amber"

Her eyes welled with tears once more. We just sat for a moment.

Shakily she spoke; "That is so sweet of you, thank you". I smiled. "Hey, I have a collection of swords at home, you just let me know who upset you", I joked. A brief smile on her face.

I realised that staff are probably not allowed to talk to patients about themselves. I took a small sip of tea, and told her what an amazing human I thought she was – a literal angel in blue. I offered to be there for her to talk to if she wanted, repeating what an amazing human I thought she was.

She thanked me. Clumsily wiped the tears from her eyes and said she had to get going.

I sat for a minute, reflecting on just how hard these people's jobs are. Their chosen profession – to be in an unpredictable workplace day-after-day. To work with people who by definition were ... "unwell" (I was going to say crazy). And yet they all report for duty every day, ready to serve. Heroes

SURPRISE EUTHANASIA

Have you ever seen videos on YouTube etc, that make you go "What the fuck was that?"? You know the ones. They leave you stunned and incapable of moving your jaw, as your brain tries to get a handle on the situation. And then the more you sit and think (maybe rewatch), the more your brain's gears start grinding to a halt and you just stare...

Well, this uhh "Chapter" is that video on paper. But, bear with me – remember that a team of psychologists and psychiatrists have thought it best to confine me to a "Specialist Mental Facility", largely because they thought my thinking was a little *off-colour*.

<u>WHAT IS "SURPRISE EUTHANASIA"?</u> Well, from my reading into places like Dignitas, you travel there, they have several discussions and meetings with you, then you finally get your family there and you are given a cocktail of drugs that take you away. The problem with it, is *that you know you are going to die*. You travelled there on a one way ticket, knowing you are not coming back.

I find it an interesting observation of the human spirit to *want to live*. Few of us want to die and even the suicidal among us rarely *want to truly die* – we mostly just want the pain to end. Whatever that pain might be...

Enter "Surprise Euthanasia" – where the patient doesn't know it is coming, and cannot see it coming. My poor wife, when I first mentioned this to her, said "So you mean murder?". But no, not murder. Murder is... well, not this. Allow me to explain;

A topic I have given some considerable thought to, is Euthanasia. If that is surprising, I can only imagine you're on your lunch rush in London, hopped into Waterstone's and picked up the first random weird "Collection of pages" that you came across – which ultimately brought you to this topic. In which case, welcome to my Insani-world...

So, Euthanasia.

It is – at its very best – a slippery ethical slope that quickly leads to raised voices and anger. Then here I am, with all the charisma of a drunkard wandering into a hornet's nest, weighing in on it...

I think that a society that does not allow for Euthanasia, is not as good, or wholesome or "advanced" in their thinking as they imagine.

Take for example pets.

Every pet owner knows the terrible privilege that they might one day have to make a decision to put their pet down. Pets – unless abused – are put down when they get too old, and their continued existence is just misery. Or they are put down when stricken with some disease or something that cannot be cured, and only leaves the poor animal in pain and suffering.

Out of love, we then – as I have – made the call to have our pets euthanised. It is a terrible thing to do, and as someone who loves their pets deeply, it is a decision reverberates in your memory for years.

But we do it, we make those decisions, because it is *inhumane* to keep the animal living in so much pain/discomfort etc. I've spoken about my own desire for euthanasia in previous chapters. But this is Euthanasia especially for humans. And this I mean with every ounce of deep empathy and compassion.

I've seen – I've eaten with, listened to, and lived with people with various mental health problems for over a month now. Thing is, this isn't even the kind of hospital for the more severe mental health cases. There are other facilities where people are detained at, that cater to some pretty intensive cases.

Still, there are one or two patients here who are really struggling. Flower is one of them. I feel so desperately sorry for her! She has been locked up in a tiny room for 2 weeks now. When she was initially admitted, she had the entire library to herself (which was unfortunate, as libraries are my sanctuary). But she was also allowed a certain sense of free movement between the library, her room and the Common Room where she ... "interacted" with us. It was a bit awkward, as she'd walk up to us at a speed faster than I can jog, with her two handlers in tow. Then she'd drool on us as she would hand out hastily drawn sketches of flowers with her name next to it – at the pace and in the style of what a 2 year old might do. Her entire behaviour was that of a 2 year old child, barely able to understand others and just really struggling with the concept of cause and effect.

Not sure if someone complained, or if the tea on the ceiling was a result of her (she has a tendency to throw stuff).

Anyway, in her case, I feel "Surprise Euthanasia" would be appropriate. And again, I say this with the deepest level of empathy and a desperately sorry heart for her. This poor woman has evidently endured some trauma that has caused her to completely regress. I'm not aware of her clinical status or prognosis. But I've heard of, and read enough research papers to know that there are patients like her, who never "get better".

Now she's locked up, and screams – *screams* – day and night until they sedate her. She normally wakes up around 6 – 7am, screaming like a banshee and banging the door much like Jean-Claude Van Damme kicking the coconut tree in Kickboxer. Waking up with that kind of racket, *and then realising you're still in the damn mental hospital*, is ... "unnerving". *Unnerving.* HA! I have become such an expert at British understatement.

Would Euthanasia in a case like that not be more *humane* for poor Flower?

She requires 3 staff members around her at all times. Until she was locked up, she upset most of the patients – myself being the only one who willingly sat for her to drool on and draw pictures for (all of which I've kept). Despite me dodging the one patient's attempt at a hug for her birthday gift, I willingly sat here whilst Flower drooled on my arm and hand and the staff just apologising for it. I smiled and said it's OK

It just seems so cruel to her. There was one night, for maybe 3 minutes, where her and I chatted ever so briefly and she was marginally able to make sense. Not sure what meds she was on. But in those 3 minutes, she kept trying to tell me she's bored, but sounded like someone who has Aphasia. Like, her brain was trying to say a thing, but her mouth kept not saying what the brain meant.

I'm no expert on Aphasia, and all I really know from it I learned on Star Trek Deep Space Nine – and that you need a Bajoran scientist to cure it.

But this poor woman. Suppose that whatever is wrong with her cannot be fixed; Does it not make more ethical sense to quietly euthanise her? A tiny drop of a certain liquid on her arm after she has taken her regular sleep tablets, and she doesn't have to wake up trapped in a body that cannot be fixed.

A prisoner in a mental cage from which there's no escape, freed from misery.

There are substances out there which just a tiny drop on exposed skin would be lethal, and they work incredibly fast. I've removed references to those, but they exist. BUT the point is that it would work reasonably quickly, and the patients would never wake back up into the nightmare cages their bodies have become.

Once you stop being all morally upset at me, and give it some thought, re-read this. Every word I wrote was with Love. A sense of mercy and desire to reduce suffering. Unending suffering.

Like I said, this isn't a unique case. I've read papers, and heard 1st hand testimonies of people who work with patients who are disabled, double-incontinent, completely "absent" in terms of mental awareness and generally do little other than existing. If at any point in your life you've argued that "the planet has limited resources", then you would surely concede the argument in this? How many families are torn apart by a sick relative, so unwell that they fall into this not-very-edge-case scenario?

Even if you don't concede on moral grounds, then consider the pure mathematics behind it. Resources, help, money, that could well be spent on other people who have a greater chance of survival could benefit.

Of course, I understand *moral* objections. Ethical objections against surprise euthanasia are just vaunted nonsense. I cannot see any ethical justification in keeping a HUMAN BEING alive in circumstances that any rational person would baulk at keeping an animal alive in.

Granted, it could be – well euthanasia is by definition a very slippery slope. At what point does a person receive the gift of surprise euthanasia? Who are the arbiters of this? How would said arbiters decide on each case?

I do not know.

And I guess that's why we in the 21st Century still fiercely argue and debate the issue.

There are many moral, legal and ethical objections to this – I realise that. I am fully aware of the complexities involved. What would the threshold be? Who gets to decide who lives and dies? How long do you observe someone before you decide? What about personal autonomy? There are endless questions as well as religious and very valid legal objections. I also realise that (at least so I am told) Animal life and Human life are not the same thing, so cannot be evaluated in the same way regarding this topic. But it still seems so utterly cruel to me to keep a human in pain bondage, when we'd release an animal out of love and "being humane".

Ultimately, the Surprise Euthanasia would simply be a mechanism to end suffering where a human being is suffering so greatly, and they cannot consent to anything. Just a sudden, painless end to misery and suffering.

I'm not denying the complexity of the issues behind this. But I am seeing the pain and suffering of humans who would really rather not suffer anymore...

THE YELLOW FLOWER (Sunday 21 May 2023)

Today I did the strangest thing. I went outside.
No reason. Just outside. Sitting on the bench in the sun.

Just sitting.

I did get off the bench to drool (almost literally) over a blue Toyota Hilux pickup truck.

On my way back to the bench, I walked the "long way" around to get to my bench – the low gradient ramp for wheelchairs. Minding where I walk, my gaze was on the ground.

Then I saw it.

The yellow flower!

Flower... I use the word reservedly. It wasn't exactly a flower – gardeners would say it is a weed. Probably is a weed, given it was the only one among the grass and given the generally unfriendly looking rest of the plant. A Meadow Buttercup (Ranunculus acris or whatever of the other names it has).

And yet; The yellow flower did not care. It did not care what humans call it. It did not care that it was a weed among the grass. It did not care that it was different. It did not care that it was yellow, and the grass green.

It could not care really – *for which plant chooses to be a rose and which chooses to be a weed*? All they are, is what they are. A gardener might rip it out, or an animal eat it – or a fat guy can walk past it on a lazy Sunday afternoon and be so taken by it, that he wrote about it.

Yet, all it did, was be a yellow flower.

Under a cloudless Welsh sky, the sun gently warmed the earth. And there, under the gentle sun, the petals were unfolded, exposed to the gentle warmth of the sun. How easily it could be harmed. How obviously it stood out from the grass – easy for an annoyed gardener to spot and rip out. Yet it did not shy away from being the best version of itself it can be.

In glorious elegance, it radiated with a stunning beauty that stopped me in my tracks. I looked at it. I took photos of it. I bent down to get better photos of it. Bent down to admire it up close.

YOU are the Buttercup. An exquisite creation, resplendent beacon in a sea of anonymity.

You can try be a rose, but it won't suit you. You can try be a daisy, but it is impossible. So just be YOU. Be who you are and never mind the rest. For we are all trying to reach out to the sun, to have our lives affirmed under a gently warming star. At the end of the day, you will find those who smell the rose. Those who admire the lavender. But there are also those who would stop to look at you, admire you and find you to be so exquisite that they sit and write pages in a book. A desperate attempt to capture your brilliance on paper. Absolutely enraptured by your splendour.

So just be you. You deserve love. You deserve admiration. For no other reason, than who you are

Meadow Buttercup

A rose it was not
A daisy it was not
A solitary yellow beacon in a sea of green
An exquisite Meadow Buttercup
It was *what it was*

Nor could it care really;
for which plant chooses to be a rose
and which chooses to be a weed?
Indeed, *who* chooses to be a rose?
Who chooses to be a weed?

Resplendent, it reflected the light of the Sun
As if to give evidence to the Star itself;
Of how beautifully it used its light
Of how strong it had grown
Of how beautiful it had become
And *in thanks* to the Sun,
Shone brightly among the green grass

Who can ask any more?
Who can demand anything else?
Who are we to judge?
Who are we to criticise when the Roses are red?
Who are we to comment when the Buttercup is yellow?
Who are we to judge?

So, shine Buttercup
Find your place in the world
You cannot be a Rose
But I did not stop to appreciate the Rose
I stopped to appreciate you.

Just be you
You will find those who look at the rose
And those who about you write prose;
A simple, beautiful Meadow Buttercup

THE BLUE TOYOTA HILUX

Sitting outside in the lazy warm sun, I heard what sounded like a powerful engine, but not a 6 or 8 cylinder. Powerful, but kind-of *utilitarian*. I looked up and was awed to see a gloriously blue, '17 reg Toyota Hilux – *Invincible* spec. Chrome grille, and big alloy wheels.

Like a moth to a flame, I was drawn up from the bench I sat on, to walk closer and closer to it. I could not stop staring. The driver seemed puzzled (this is a mental hospital...) that someone would – mouth agape – dawdle ever closer to his beautiful machine.

We ended up having a pretty good conversation. It's amazing the levels of depths men can communicate to other men with, knowing we're under the relatively safe umbrella in a place like this. Outside the premises, men are pressured to be iron men. In an evermore confusing world, we are faced with challenges to who we are. Challenged about what we are, how we need to behave. But here, this random guy spoke to a random mental health patient who walked up to his pickup truck like a zombie transfixed by fresh meat.

And what a conversation it was.

It started with the older gentleman saying *"Hello"* in a friendly, disarming way. Asked if I am a patient here, and I just simply said "Yes I am". Slowly he admitted that he had been here once before. Pain etched my face in empathy. Then more freely, he clarified that, not only had he visited here before, he had once been a patient here as well. I tilted my head left, and raised an eyebrow in curiosity – inviting him to elaborate.

He had a deep struggle with depression. His wife divorced him, he lost his farm. But, he said "I am doing much better now". Though I do not doubt that he's doing better, the pain in his voice was evident. All I could muster was a sheepish "I am *so sorry*".

Awkward silence

Then I asked if he's visiting someone. "A lady from church", he said.

His eyes instantly recognisable to what I have seen here in the ward so many times – really mostly with men. I speak to the women and men fairly equally, maybe slightly more with the women actually. But the women have not once, not one of them, had this almost far-off, distant stare as their voice trails off. It's something I've really just noticed in the men here. The emotional pain that overwhelms them and makes their eyes get lost in the distance. How interesting.

Anyway, he got *the stare* and with deep notes of pain said "*It's hard when you're in church and depressed. People just don't understand*". He caught himself almost instantly, apologised, and again repeated that he's feeling a lot better. Almost as if to convince himself, I thought.

"Yes, people don't understand how hard this is when you're part of a church", I offered. Not, dear reader, that you should consider me any example of Christianity. In fact, forget that. If you think of exactly what a Christian should not be like, then that's me. Don't judge Christians by the poor example I set.

What stayed with me even more than the exquisite mechanical beast the man arrived in, were his words about people in church not understanding.

That is tragic. If you think about it – if you read the Gospel of Jesus, you'd *expect* the most broken people to be in church. The good ones and the ones who have a handle on life should be out doing their thing. Church should have been for the broken people. But I guess there are practical reasons that broken people like me ought to be in hospitals like this instead of in church with good people.

But the gist of what the Hilux Man said (or didn't say), is how at church we're so often *expected* to be happy. *Expected* to be in a cheery, celebratory mood. I hesitate to add "because of the Joy of the Lord" – but that's the truth. And when you don't feel like that, when you still *actively plan your suicide* despite people praying for you, that's when the judgement starts. Sideways glances. Whispers of being demon-possessed. Which you know, if someone is in such a desperate, dark place that they are planning on how to end their lives – and are accused of being demon-possessed – is pretty shitty. You have no idea how awful a situation it is until you're in it.

And if you are one of those good church people who are so happy, and you take issue with the previous paragraph; Please sit down, and shut up.

Please.

It's *exactly at this point*, that you should be a bit more introspective and ask yourself if you have ever treated a person like this. Not just suicidal mugs like me. Anyone. And then just realise that it is so hurtful and more likely to affirm to someone that they ought to end their life when you suggest they are not spiritual enough – or whatever religious piety you aspire to..

Half a lifetime ago, I used to be a lay-preacher. I used to regularly preach at 3 or so churches, who used to invite me. I recall one day there was a massive plane crash I think in Indonesia or thereabouts. There was an article published in the church paper [about the tragedy], and by sheer happenstance, I was near a group of congregation members who were discussing it. They agreed, among the five of them, that the plane crash was God's punishment for getting on a plane and not going to church.

Hearing these ladies discuss how God punishes people who sin by not going to church – and a number of other instances with different people from the same church – I decided it's time to depart.

After all, hell man, look how many times I've sworn in this "*Not a Book*" already. There's evidently little place for filthy sinners like me. Plus my encouragement of "Surprise Euthanasia" – geesh, most people will likely say I am damned either way. And yet, I am just trying (and failing miserable I admit) to navigate Life. Even my appalling stance on Euthanasia is born out of a broken heart for those with broken spirits and bodies.

Ironically, I've found more love, care, understanding and support from agnostic people than church goers. I once did a sermon, which I was poignantly reminded of recently, where I said that "One of the biggest problems with Christians, is that *they pray too much*".

By this, I meant (and this was from observational evidence), people would "pray for the upcoming church camp". But only ever the same five or ten people would pitch up, roll up their sleeves and put in hours of work to prepare. Oh, the others would "Pray for you", before going about their day, piously satisfied that they've done their duty by offering a quick 17 second prayer.

Meantime, back at the farm, it's only ever the same handful of people who truly rock up to do the work. Who prepare meals, who serve others, who wash dishes. And often – how funny is this – they were the ones who deemed themselves *most unworthy of love and redemption* that did the work. The "good ones" just did their few seconds of prayer, and wear fancy hats to church, stuff their faces with shared lunch, then complain about how bad the food was, or how little of it there was.

NOW, I FEEL I NEED TO ADD HERE THAT I AM BEING VERY UNFAIR. I APOLOGISE.

This particular story is largely focused around my intimate interactions with one or two denominations. In the more modern, "happy clappy" charismatic type denominations, this is much less of an issue.

In fact, the church my wife and I attend (~2023) has been particularly good at – well, praying yes – but also arriving on the scene and doing the hard, difficult sweaty work. I've been so surprised at seeing the demographic spread in cars alone. Mercedes, BMW, Porsche, even a Maserati among the other cars – owners who are clearly well off and not "needing church as a crutch".

But these people, despite being so wealthy, pitch up on the scene, do hours and hours of work in adverse weather for people. Not for the church, but to help other people. And not out of pious self-righteousness either – a genuine, warm, loving compassion and wanting to give to others and to help.

Actually, as I write this, a couple or three names immediately spring to mind. I won't embarrass them by using their names in my "Not book", but man, what amazing people.

Anyway, I give churches and church people a lot of grief, because I feel they ought to know better. "Judge not, lest ye be judged" and all?

I've often said to people that I wish I could start a church for broken people. No good, perfect people allowed. Just a place where broken, hurt, damaged people can go and find healing for their souls. Find acceptance with others – like the acceptance I've found with fellow patients here. Everyone recognising they're *here* for a start, here for a reason.

I realise the bitter irony and hypocrisy in this if you look at what I've previously said. Especially about shouting at the one woman who sang to comfort herself. But I am slowly learning and realising that judging others does nobody any good.

After all, even the best of us can only be bent and broken so many times before our precious "House of cards" tumbles down.

I've often thought of certain "perfect" people I know, and then looked at fellow patients. Wondered if those "perfect" individuals with their vaunted superiority would have been able to remain standing if they had to endure some of the awful that patients here have had to deal with.

If you are one of those pious, wonderful people who sneer at broken assholes like me, just be glad you've not had to deal with the same crap we've had to deal with, with the resources we've had to cope with. Who knows, if you did, you might not still be standing...

Scheduled Maintenance

Cars! Interesting machines
A - B they conduct us safely
Work hard to run the AC
Play is music on the way
And in a crash, self-sacrifice for our safety

In return they need so little
Some fuel for power
Some oil on occasion
And a service when pipes become brittle

RUBBISH CAR!
We're quick to curse
When a tyre bursts
Or it breaks down

Yet we took loyalty for granted
Whilst we ignored service calls
When we ignored new tyre warnings
When we did not give the little it needed

Think human instead of car;
How we take people for granted
The loyal Golden Retriever personality
Who loyally stands by your side;

Despite your constant neglect
Despite your constant kicks
Kicks in punishment for what others did
Neglect in light of what others did

So you neglect your human,
Like you did your car
You take for granted your human,
Like you did your car

And when their souls finally break?
You berate and slander
You gossip and mock
Yet you were the one who could have helped

Next time your car breaks down,
Next time your human breaks -
Blame not their mind or engine
Blame instead who should have maintained
Look in the mirror, you're the cause of the pain

THE JOB INTERVIEW (Thursday 18 May)

Not just a job interview; *The Job Interview*. The *Final* Interview

I had strength in me for one last cavalry charge. To pick up my sword for the last time, hands drenched in blood and mud. My sword feels heavy in my arms, blade chipped from many fights. For one last time, I was able – forced myself to muster strength. Muster strength like trying to scoop water from a depleted pool. I did what was required, and fought with every final ounce of strength. My body is finished, my mind all but spent.

One final battle I fought. Blood-mud grinding between my hand and the sword. My shield, broken and ruined. Every final ounce of vitality I had is spent. I have no more.

In blissful ignorance, I slipped into unconsciousness. Now I just wait; Yeah or Nay will determine if I live another day.

****

It went OK. I finished at 3pm, and slept most of the afternoon until 8pm. I am absolutely exhausted.

A week to 2 weeks to hear back. So it's the long wait – which is hard. Just want it over already. The Lead Engineer and I didn't get along. It was tough, he asked questions but actually meant something wholly different. Plus both the people who interviewed me haven't even joined the company yet. So I wait...

My stay in hospital is at least extended until Tuesday/Thursday next week.

I'm glad the hospital stay has been extended. Some extra "safe" time. My oldest son finished University today – he's moving out in August

My youngest moves out in September. And my wife is so busy with her Master's Degree in Psychology, she hardly has time to talk.

If you wanted to argue against suicide on the basis of selfishness – firstly do not. It is such a stupid, base argument – and so fucking insulting to someone contemplating suicide. As if their burden is not already so great that their spirits are crushed – to add to that accusations of selfishness?!? FUCKING ASSHOLE YOU ARE!

But if you have to, an argument can be made that I am of much more use of the hospital staff and especially the patients here than at home. In fact, all things considered, I have more human connection and conversations here. I keep sitting on my ugly yellow chair, and patients keep coming to sit by me and talking to me. Or we just sit quietly. It's up to them how much we talk or don't and a LOT of people have said to me I am like the counsellor here that helps them. Again, tragically ironic given how messed up I am.

So I suspect my imminent death will be a greater shock and distress for my fellow patients and ward staff.

But hey

Only if Death is literally standing in the corner of *your* room, scythe sharp and ready to reap your soul, and his ice cold breath chills your bones, you'll know what it's like. Only once you have walked this dark path, will you know what it's like. And if you never did- or never will wrestle with Life and Death like this, then count yourself lucky

Fighting to stay alive has been hard.

Anyway, I kinda think Death has won here – just need that final NO from the interview and wham – done. As for right now, Friday 19 May at 1:53am, I am going to bed and not getting up. I mean not to get up at all except for medication. The rest of the time, I will be in *hyperspace* – trying to not have awful dreams. But the sleep will be good

Signing out for probably the last time, as I plan to not write anymore.

If the Job is a NO, then I execute Order 66 and die. Not leaving notes or contrived nonsense. I think the Collection of Pages here are more than sufficient to highlight my daily struggle with pain, and especially my struggles with self-worth. Actually, I might just pull the proverbial trigger regardless of the job...

Thank you for reading. Nico Weyers, signing off

FINAL HOURS (Monday 22 May)

I need to write fast now, not much time left to write. The day has dawned on what might likely be my final week.

I had an obscenely bad night. I was in so much pain all day yesterday. DESPITE 15mg of Zopiclone sleep tablets the hospital gave me, I could not get to sleep. The pain was so bad, I could not breathe. In fact, for the past month of my *incarceration* here, I have slept without my sleep apnoea machine, mostly really to avoid people needing to sit and watch me while I sleep.

Because I am on Suicide Watch, I am checked every 15 minutes. I am not allowed to have cables in my room – lest I strangle myself. So if I have the sleep apnoea machine, people need to sit in 1 hour shifts, and watch me sleep, which is awkward. So I have been going without my machine.

But last night I was in such desperate pain, unable to breathe, that at 2 am the nurses were helping me set up the machine. I woke up a few times, and then around 5am woke up groaning from pain.

The reason I start this chapter with paragraphs of redundant pain description, is to highlight that nothing has changed since I got here 4 weeks ago today. I am still in intolerable pain day and night. My initial stay here, whilst "voluntary" became a forced incarceration. I am fed up. I broke bones in my hands from punching the concrete walls. Not sure why. I have bruises on my forehead from hitting myself hard in the head with a walking stick. I am clearly in a worse mental state now than when I got here.

So, with all this pain, I am just so finished. I cannot anymore.

If the interview feedback is a NO, *then that's it*. My death being a gift to my family and society.

I've got what I need to get the job done – despite 2 random room searches (one of which was without me in the room to hide stuff), my equipment is still concealed and nobody knows of it. Well you do now because you are reading this. But at the time of writing, nobody knows. Don't get the staff in trouble though. It's not their fault. They normally deal with people who might be suicidal, but not maybe who have planned as well as I have. And despite there being no opportunity to get things to me – I have planned ahead. Far ahead. Hell, back in March when I was only here for a week, I had this awful thought that I might be back. So I planned. I am not exactly on the stupid end of the intelligence spectrum, so you cannot blame people for not finding things that I shouldn't have had. Please do not blame them. This is all 100% on me, and me alone.

I am in so much pain today. Have I said this yet?

I cannot go on existing like this.

The Powys NHS as an organisation clearly either doesn't really care, or is just so hopelessly slow that it pretty much doesn't matter. Hell, even just some nice good pain relief would have helped so much. They've denied surgery which could have fixed it. When I had one messed up disc in my spine, they could have fixed it. I have 4 desiccated discs now. I've lost over 2cm in height.

Instead of some decent pain management, all I had were increasingly high doses of morphine for 4 ½ years until that almost killed me. Then it was withdrawn, to a point now where I have almost nothing. And nothing new is apparently forthcoming for – and I quote verbatim "Several months". And even several months means that it would be a gradual ramp-up from a situation that became unbearable years ago.

Ethically, this is on the NHS in many ways. Not this particular hospital's staff – they are some of the most amazing humans I've ever met. But the decision makers, the ones who didn't take the 3rd degree burns from hot water bottles as a sign that I was in great pain.

And in an unexpected twist, they are sending me home today without warning. Clearly, even here I have outstayed my welcome, like a turd floating in the toilet

FINAL WEEK
Dawn
My final week
Nobody knows
blissfully ignorant, they think I'm fine
with others I laugh as we wine and dine
None aware my time is gone

Should my interview be a No
Then I am fully prepared to Go
Go where nobody can follow
Go where no pain can reach
Go where I can find Peace

Many feel Suicide is unforgivable
But I believe;
Father's eyes would be filled with tears
That His child was still in pain after all these years
And so with open arms
Hold me tight
When my days were dark as night
And my spirit could not suffer any more

Those who stay behind;
Do not think in your hearts I am unkind
For deciding to depart
For being weak in the face of pain
For failing
Failing.
Falling, and failing.
My body is broken
My spirit is broken

I have tried
I have failed
Spectacularly so
Death is my punishment
Death is my freedom

THE JOB IS A NO (Thursday 25 May 2023)

At the start of this week, I woke up with a deep realisation that my last week had dawned.

A big deciding factor was that I'd make the decision once I hear about the job.

Today I heard back, and it's a NO from the job.

SO that's it then. The end of my story. Tonight – sadly at home – my life ends.

Peace to you

Greater men have died for less
And here I am in the final analysis
A life reasonably thoroughly lived
A life now utterly without worth

Without a job
Without an income
Without worth
Without worth

My wife concerned
Sell her house?
Or live in a van?
Barely big enough for a mouse

So I take my leave
Do not cry for me
This Peace I needed anyway

Lord, please take your lost child
Please take your child who is afraid
Please take the child who is utterly broken

Peace to you

THIS IS AWKWARD… (27 May 2023, 2:14am)

I think the only story with more endings, was Lord of the Rings; Return of the King. So, no more goodbyes – I've said my piece. From hereon out, I'll only be adding small increments to the tragic comedy that is my life.

THE HORNET IN THE BOURBON

There once was a guy in Wales
Who wrote of his bullshit tales
Entered a hornet into the room
And gently trying to save it from doom

But the fat guy was a moron
Because he had drunk some bourbon
And in that glass caught the hornet
Who drank heartily from the bourbon

A drunken hornet is a thing to see
Three times larger than a bee
Buzzing in the glass from the bourbon
Bouncing drunken in the glass to get free

FRIDAY 9 JUNE 2023 – Last quick update

I built my LEGO castle. What an enjoyable set. Definitely get it if you have been toying with the idea. It's a great set to build!

Anyway... Yeah, I am still here for now. I realised that my poor mother was in Thailand on holiday for her birthday. I didn't want to wreck her holiday.

I also realised my son is going to Croatia on a much-anticipated holiday from 9 – 16 June. It's been a big consideration, he's been so excited.

But now, AT LAST, it is *my* time. I've planned and marked 19 June – 2 July as my "Green Zone" time. That is the only really safe time I can commit suicide without ruining someone's special something. The 3rd *would have been* my 45th birthday. But my family will save some money on my birthday from hereon out ☺

I've carefully considered and planned this. It's kinda sad that I'd be dead, as I would have *loved* to have heard doctors and coroners remark on how very intelligently, and cleverly I've planned this suicide.

It's brilliant;

Basically, I don't want to cause trauma to First Responders (I might have said that previously), so don't want to make a bloodied mess. Nor do I want to ruin my home or car – and frankly that excludes a LOT of options.

So I turned to science. Dear Coroner, here's how I did it.

I have decided to use CONSTRUCTIVE WAVEFORM INTERFERENCE.

So there it is. My clever plan, using Constructive Waveform interference.

I really do not belong anywhere, or church or town or Life anymore. I previously stood at the edge of a precipice.

But now, I realise the Buffet of Life has been thoroughly sampled, and it's just going to be shitty from hereon out. So time to leave the table so to speak.

It's a happy event – I'd have people celebrate that I am free from all the different forms of pain... Face it; I was a factory mistake and should never have been born. I am fixing that problem by giving my family and Earth the gift of my death. No longer am I going to be a lodestone around their necks. My family free to live their lives.

People can live in freedom without me darkening their doorframes

I am looking forward to my dying day. Just need to wait for a rainy day before 3 July and I am out of here. Certainly do not want to reach 45 years of age...

So there it is. A final note. Hope the coroners and doctors appreciate the care and thoroughness of my planning ☺

May 2024 – a year later; Attempt details redacted for safety of others, and to avoid giving others ideas and inspiration. This "writing" was around my struggles in life and my own issues with mental health. It was not to serve as a way to help others end their lives. So in the interest of the safety of others, I chose to redact this part

The Hurricane

Weak house!
Pathetic dolphin!
Useless boat!
Stupid human!

The walls of the house collapsed
Once protecting its occupants
Suddenly washed away by the flood
The Hurricane asked in the maelstrom;
"Why weren't you stronger where you stood?"

Confusion filled the dolphin
Swimming in the ocean
Suddenly yeeted into the sky
The Hurricane asked in the wind;
"Why can you not fly?"

Engulfed by titanic waves
Sailing majestically across the ocean
Against monstrous waves, naught but a mote
The Hurricane asked in the cataclysm;
"Why could you not just float?"

Horror filled the human
All around catastrophe and disaster
Lost in the Eye of the Storm
The human looked up and asked;
"Why cause all the destruction?"

The I of the storm...
Innocent is Me
I caused none of it
It's the fault of all those around
Little does the Hurricane see
It caused all the disaster to those who mourn

Little do we see that we're the Eye
We're the I
The I who causes the storm
The I who blames everyone else
We don't use our Eye to see the I
To see the disasters that in our wakes lie

SATURDAY 17 JUNE

One of my most favourite movies is *The Equalizer* with Denzel Washington. One scene, the girl (Alina) is greeted by Denzel's character with some birthday cake. He points out to Alina (referring to off-screen conversations) that she was meant to give up refined sugar, as it's bad for her vocal chords – and asks when she plans on giving up. Clearly beat from a tough day, she dejectedly replies *"Any day now"*.

You, the reader, are Denzel Washington, and I am Alina. With disbelief and justified annoyance you ask "I thought you were meant to be dead by now?". To which my reply is *"Any day now..."*. I still mean to go through with it. Especially after this weekend.

During my many conversations with Psychiatrists, Psychologists et al, I stated unequivocally that I have no more value in life. I am a burden to my family, I've done nothing of value and that my *existence* is worth less than that of a virus. It's sad and comforting to know that I was right.

It's June. FUCKING MID-JUNE. And I've done fuck all but shit and sleep. Like a jellyfish without a spine. Just like Mrs Potgieter told me in my 4th year of Primary School.

In my defence (and I know it is lame); I've survived. I mean it is of fuckall worth, but it feels like an achievement. To one of the points my wife raised; I've squandered months of having time and luxury to improve myself. But consider for a moment, that I had no plans to exist beyond end May. I've actively been planning on *ending my useless life*. Why would I put in any effort to "improving" my life if I am planning on ending it?

I baulk at the word "Improve" in context of my life. Putting lipstick on a pig is of greater worth than "improving" this ... *existence*. Why would I waste resources, other people's time and energy and even basic water on improving a situation I've actively been planning on ending? I feel like such an arsehole for saying this. Or thinking this. Or feeling like this. But there it is.

Cruel irony. I am beset by a bitterly cruel irony. A friend has, what might end up being terminal cancer. She's (outwardly) taking it well, going for tests etc and seeming fine with whatever the result is. The irony here, is that *she has value*. Her life *has value*. She does so much good – objectively good, wonderful, life-affirming things for others. And yet she's likely dying. Then there's me, who has 0 value. Actually, it's far on the minus scale – my value. A zero would have been an improvement... Anyway, me whose life stopped being worth anything at all, living. Continuing to live despite even trying suicide.

Fuck, Life is cruel and filled with bitter irony. Those who want to live cannot, and those who want to die cannot. It's not even just this instance – it's a cruelty I've observed all my life. People, some of the most wonderful souls to occupy a body, who so desperately want children, but cannot conceive. Then there are those who fuck around and dispose of inconvenient pregnancies with less care and thought than disposing of an empty Coke can.

FUCK. LIFE.

Of course the other unspoken irony here, is that people wish they had the luxury of having 5+ months off work, 2 of which are spent in the relative comfort and safety of a mental hospital – in order to improve themselves in some way. Learn Russian, or become the next Picasso or whatever. Then fat fuck Nico who did naught but sulk and waste oxygen. Where others might have killed for the same privilege, I squandered it. I am evidently an ungrateful cunt. Very much undeserving of life.

VERY. MUCH. UNDESERVING. OF. LIFE.

I'll fix it soon$^{(tm)}$ though. Isn't it weird? I am so hell-bent on ending my life, so hell-bent on not being a burden anymore – yet I continuously put other people's needs ahead of my own desire to die. It's not an excuse either; I didn't want to defile other people's

special dates or events. Like my son's trip to Croatia, which he thoroughly enjoyed. Seemed wrong to ruin that. But as (my hopefully final) Father's Day is about to dawn, I am entering "a green zone" that I marked in my calendar. The only date I stand to ruin is the wretched anniversary of my birth, which really deserves to be ruined.
Like I said at the start of this chapter; Any day now

SYNAESTHESIA...

There is one thing I like about myself. Synaesthesia. I was in my late thirties when I discovered that not everybody "hears colour", or "sees taste". Synaesthesia is a neurological condition – interestingly, a trait "that is almost three times higher in people with [Autism]". Interesting correlation...

Synaesthesia has multiple different presentations. But essentially, it boils down to the senses in the brain being "cross-wired". In real world terms, it means that if I listen to a piece of music, I "hear" colour. Ludovico Einaudi is an interesting example of a composer whose music is composed almost exclusively of pastel colours. Hues of pink and yellow mostly. Whereas Bittersweet Symphony by Blur is one of the only purple songs I know.

Number 5 is blue. Exactly #1520A6 / RGB: 21, 32, 166.

Mondays are red, Fridays are shiny black, like a thick treacle made from shiny obsidian.

Lipton's Early Grey Tea smells like an orange pyramid when dry, but turns into an olive green dodecahedron.

Yeah, it's weird. People I've spoken to have asked me if I am on [name of drug] (LDS or mushrooms), as apparently that is how it sounds. But that's how my brain processes sensory input. Granted it's weird – but it has allowed me to experience, and enjoy life in ways most people cannot understand. Which is great.

One of the groups playing with colour in my mind at the moment is "Of Monsters and Men" – damn great group, with amazing music.

It's so weird to think people don't hear colour or taste shapes. Much I guess like trying to explain to someone blind from birth what blue or red looks like. Synaesthesia is such a profoundly wonderful sensation, but so impossible to accurately communicate

CHANGE OF TACK (Sunday 18 June)

Whilst I have been dead-set on ending my own miserable existence, I realised yesterday that this *Not a Book* might not just be read by psychiatrists and psychologists in an effort to understand how someone can go off the deep end. I doubt many people who commit suicide write a bloody book about it first. Sure, those *who survive* tell stories of "Hope" (LOL) and recovery.

But I have not seen much material from those planning on ending their lives. Unless Google et al suppress it?

I realised though, that there might be families and loved ones who are looking for answers, trying to understand what went on in those final hours and how it got that bad. Why their loved ones never said anything before ending their lives. So I thought I'd add some of my own input. In fear of being the useless *Dick on a Donkey* I mentioned earlier, please see this chapter purely as an attempt to maybe help you.

I will try unpack it as carefully as I can;

I guess the first thing to explain here, is that I really take issue with the phrase "Commit Suicide". I used the phrase often, but really because that is the phrase that we as a culture use. The word "Commit" is the one I take issue with here.

As if it is a crime...

I disagree wholeheartedly that it is a crime.

If you have never been in a situation so bad that you thought of ending your life, please; *COUNT YOURSELF LUCKY*. Humans are some of the finest expressions of Life.

It might be that in our Solar System, or our local Galaxy – *or even the Universe* – that humans are the only intelligent life that exists. Mull over that point a bit. It might well be that in all the vastness of space – be it local or inter-galactic, there is no other planet with beings on that can create music. Or paint great paintings, or create sculptures and statues with their hands. We might well be – Earth might well be – the only place and people in the Universe who can *think*. Who can *love*. That is no small thing. Imagine the Universe existing and only on this planet can rational thought and beauty be found.

People often anger me online when they "sell humanity out". Places like YouTube videos that talk about Intelligent Life, or the Fermi Paradox – they say that "Aliens don't visit because there's no intelligent life on Earth" etc. As if Alien life in whatever form it takes (if it exists), is somehow more worthy, more capable of love, hope, compassion than we are. No dear reader, HUMANS are beautiful creatures. Don't sell us out on account of a few bad apples.

My point here, is that Humans are amazing creatures. Capable of so much Hope, Compassion, Love, Empathy and all other good things. We have a built-in drive to *live life*, and to hope beyond hope that tomorrow will be a better day. Prisoners of war have survived, slaves have survived – people still survive daily in some of the worst conditions imaginable, because of HOPE. Hope that they will be freed. Hope that things will get better. Hope that tomorrow will be better.

AND YET

Those who ultimately decide to end their lives see no hope.

Can you imagine that? Sit for a moment and think of how we as a species have so much hope, that we have survived some truly appalling circumstances.

YET, *your loved one saw so little hope, that they ended their lives*. That is no small thing! It is frankly a tragic situation to be in. To have so little *Hope*, that all you can think to do, the only *"viable"* choice, being to end your own life. And it's not easy. Trust me. Getting to that decision took many, many **dark days**. Dark thoughts. Unsettling thoughts. Planning. Figuring out how to end a life. Being in the UK, I don't have access to guns, so couldn't shoot myself in the head with a Colt .45. Being a pussy who doesn't want to harm others, I did not want to traumatise train drivers for example by stepping in front of a train (and then disrupting the rail network and making people late for their important appointments). I did also not want to traumatise *First Responders* by leaving a bloodied corpse. So I had to try figure out, and plan a way to end my life in a way that will 1) be successful, 2) be away from home so that I did not traumatise my family and 3) Not traumatise or leave too much of a mess for others.

For MONTHS, that is what my thoughts and mental energy went into.

Not improving myself.

And when the NHS locked me up in a mental hospital for over 6 weeks, all I could think of, was to play it "sane" like *Sarah Connor* in Terminator 2. Try to impress the doctors and nursing staff with big, fancy keywords that communicated to them that I was fine, all was fine and they should let me go.

My wife is angry with me for not spending time to improve myself. For not spending time with God to improve my spiritual life. For not taking time to learn a new skill, or a new trade.

How could I?
What is the point?

My thoughts have been solely on ending my life. Improving myself? FOR WHAT? Seriously. Why? If your every waking thought is about ending your life, why would you learn Mandarin, or study Calculus? OK, wait, I take back the Calculus thing – I love Space and all related things, and Calculus helps understand Space better. But beyond that, really no point eh?

And growing spiritually? Let me tell you that I have zero plan to do that. I do not feel worthy to stand in a church. Or to stand before the Cross and ask for forgiveness. I don't feel worthy to even be alive – how would I go to God and seek His favour and blessing?

Indeed, as someone put it; I am "*clearly demon-possessed*" – so why would I go to church? If I am so filthy and so worthless that I am demon-possessed, what place do I have in a church with good church people??

And at this point, allow me to pause as well. Telling someone who has so little Hope – that they want to end their lives – *that they are demon possessed? ARE YOU FUCKING JOKING?* Really? That is the most helpful thing in your arsenal? Someone who is so destroyed, so flat, so drained and empty, you say they are demon possessed?

Maybe church people just have a different outlook. All I know is that to me, that is not a helpful comment to make. Indeed, quite the opposite… But what would I know? I am just a demon possessed suicidal maniac after all…

It occurs to me I went slightly off-topic. But even in this, you can see the tremendous hurt and damage people cause to those in situations where someone is so suicidal.

FALL OF THE TITAN (22 June 2023, 21:00)

On Sunday 19 June, a submersible with 5 souls onboard dived to explore the wreck of Titanic. A ship for which I have a great deal of love and fondness for.

The Titan, a mini submersible dived and 2 hours into the dive sent an emergency message to the mothership. Since Sunday, I have been hoping, quietly praying, that the rescuers and first responders would find the Titan, and rescue those onboard. But I know enough about the great depths and the pressure where Titanic lies, to know it was unlikely they could be saved. The best case for those poor people, would be a catastrophic implosion, where they would have been killed instantly by the unimaginable pressure.

Tonight the world was informed that a catastrophic implosion had indeed occurred, likely on Sunday already when the emergency message was sent. Whilst utterly tragic, it was a better end than some of the other possibilities – especially a long, protracted suffocation in the dark, freezing depths.

A solitary tear ran down my cheek. Like rain in a dried up river bed, the first tear made it easier for the next to follow. The second tear ran faster, then a floodgate of tears followed. Deep sorrow at the loss of five human lives. Despite not knowing any of them, I've empathised so deeply, I've hoped so desperately for their safe return. Yet in knew in my heart that survival was unlikely, so I hoped for a swift death, to spare them the heartache and trauma of a slow, drawn-out death. Thankfully, mercifully, the Titan imploded. They would have been dead before they knew what had happened.

I cried when I heard the news. Tears rolled down my cheek, which I tried to hide in embarrassment. After all, I didn't know any of those people. I didn't even know they existed. And yet, here I am – crying over the loss of 5 souls in the deep, dark, unforgiving depth. WHY!? WHY DO I CRY OVER THE DEATH OF 5 PEOPLE I'VE NEVER MET?? Why do these things affect me so much?

On Saturday, driving back from Manchester, I saw someone hit a bird with their car. The bird flopped and desperately tried to fly and tried to recover. Unfortunately, traffic was so bad, I could not stop. It was so traumatic to see that. It upset me so deeply. If I could, I'd have ripped my heart out. I cannot cope with the cruelty and tragedy I witness. How am I so very weak?

Hamish Harding, Paul-Henry Nargeolet, Shahzaada Dawood, Suleman Dawood, Stockton Rush - Your legacy has been fused with Titanic. May you rest in peace a mile off Titanic's bow. And may the world leave you and the site in peace.

To those lost in the Titan, I offer my heartfelt condolences. To the families of those left behind, I offer my deepest sympathies. To those who rushed to the scene, I offer my utmost respect and gratitude. Fighting against an unforgiving ocean, in the hope of saving lives of people they've never met. You are heroes.

ODE TO A TITAN

A submersible called Titan
22 feet of technology meant to explore
Is tragically no more
Diving to the site of the wreck -
Five souls on board, eager to explore

What befell the tiny boat we may never know
The wreckage now scattered at the bow
At the feet of its once-great namesake
For the five souls on board there is peace now

It was over in an instant
Death came before any realised
Death was painless
Death was instant
In a moment of utter tragedy
At least that is a small solace!

Hamish Harding
Paul-Henry Nargeolet
Shahzaada Dawood
Suleman Dawood
Stockton Rush
Your legacy has been fused with Titanic
Your graves a mile from her bow
Your memory will endure now

My heart breaks for you
A sadness I can hardly contain
If I could give my life to save yours
I'd have it given without refrain
Be at peace
The world will always remember you

Titanic, most beautiful
Titanic, which haunts the hearts and minds

Titanic, as famous now as she has always been
You've claimed five more souls
May you now be left in peace
A resting place for souls lost at sea

And for those souls I pray
Lord, take them away
Lord, give their families peace this day
Lord, give us peace
Grant us the mercy of calm
Though we did not know them
We mourn in empathy
And let the *great ship Titanic claim no more lives*

IT'S ALIVE! (27 June 2023)

Molten plastic flows at 215° onto the print bed. I HAVE FIXED MY 3D PRINTER!

For months, it just stood there. A symbol of my failure in life. The last thing I printed was the Mothership from the game Homeworld. I used an "ironing" technique to smooth the final layer and it came out exceptionally beautiful. But sadly, the nozzle and entire heated element got clogged up.

The fix was not simple. I had to open up the hot end assembly, heat it up to melt the clogged plastic, then remove it. Surprisingly, 215° is quite hot! My fingers know this...

I first opened the hot end casing, in order to reveal the nozzle and feeder mechanism. I was surprised to see the enormous amount of plastic that ended up getting clogged in the nozzle assembly. No wonder it did not work. I took some fine pliers, and removed the heated plastic from around the casing. Then I fed a tiny wire through the heated nozzle to remove the plastic stuck inside there. I was delighted when the wire came out all the way out of the nozzle – an early sign that I was successful.

I then added some new plastic (called PLA) and fed it through the nozzle. The excitement that a tiny stream of molten plastic filled me with is impossible to convey. After months of being useless, the printer is now working. I even packed my tools away neatly in order to reflect my now improved, disciplined mental state.

I then successfully printed a magical little thing; An egg similar to the "Kinder Chocolate Eggs". Only, this has a hinge printed inside the egg, which actually works and allows you to open the egg. Once open, it contains a little F14 Tomcat plane, with working swing wings. There is no assembly required – the gear to swing the wings is printed and contained inside the plane. IT IS MAGICAL! I love it.

NOW, on balance, fixing a stupid 3d printer is hardly worth mentioning. Doesn't really mean anything, nor does it add much value to anyone's life.

Nor does it add much to my life. Only, it does add a lot. IT ADDED A LOT OF VALUE TO MY LIFE.

It showed me that I can fix things. After soaking up space for months, standing there useless, my 3d printer is now working again. AND I FIXED IT. I applied some discipline, I faced the problem, I took the tools I had and fixed it. Despite not having all the right tools, and not having a perfect environment to work in, I succeeded. I am so proud of myself.

Which leads me to the question; If I could fix a 3d printer, can I fix my life?? Maybe... Just maybe.

I mean life is not perfect. I doubt anyone's life is perfect. Like Dostoevsky so eloquently stated; Life is suffering. To live is to suffer. I am paraphrasing a lot here. But the fundamental point, is that one suffers in Life. I am very guilty of not coping well with my suffering. I am very guilty of not handling my burden well.

Problem 1;
My life, like my 3d printer, has been pretty broken. Unlike my 3d printer, my life isn't easily fixable. My spine – my back – still hurts. When I injured my back, I had 1 desiccated disc between L4 and L5. Now I have desiccated discs between L1 and L2, L2 and L3, L3 and L4 as well as L4 and L5. Also, between L5 and S1 there is some kind of issue and arthritis. And also my lumbar spine is straightening, which is not good.

So my back pain remains.

Problem 2;
I still do not have a job. I do not have an income. As a result, I feel utterly useless. I don't know how to justify my existence anymore to be honest. And I am trying man. Daily, I send out job applications. It doesn't matter if I am on the toilet, or bath, or sitting outside in the

sun – I apply for jobs. But I have NOTHING coming up. I've registered my own Company in order to maybe get contract jobs – but nothing. I am in such a deep pit of despair for the lack of work.

So my lack of work remains.

YET, SOMEHOW, I AM FEELING VAGUELY OPTIMISTIC THIS MORNING.

I feel like the 3d printer is a good metaphor for my life. I was able to sit and fix it. There were tools I used, and I took some discipline, and I fixed it. Can I fix my life like I did my printer? I certainly hope so. I kinda feel like I can, you know?

Today feels like a new start for me. Which is a feeling I've not had in ages. I feel like I can accomplish things – and that is more positive than I have felt in months.

MENTAL HEALTH DISCRIMINATION (27 June)

"Buckle your seatbelt Dorothy – Kansas is going bye-bye" – an apt intro to the discrimination against those who struggle with mental health.

Western civilisation is not as advanced as you'd think. It's not as advanced or open minded as some of the "Social Justice Warriors" would think.

In fact, I think Western Civilisation is downright savage.

As you have read by now, I've been unemployed for months. I've been looking for work. Back in early May, I participated in a podcast and spoke quite openly about my mental health issues and being Sectioned. I had a suspicion that it would affect my future career prospects.

The gentleman who hosted the podcast discussed this with me and we agreed that I'd probably not want to work for anyone who discriminates against people based on Mental Health. Naively, I thought that it would be a very small pool of people who would not discriminate.

Today I heard about a job which seemed very promising. I am perfectly qualified, I have all the experience needed, but they have been coy and giving me a cold shoulder. I just assumed they were busy. Turns out, they don't want to employ me, because of my mental health history. Really? Has this Director never been unwell?

More concerning; Am I forever now dipped in shit because I had mental health issues? Things I've worked hard to overcome, I am still being penalised for?

Talk about a dick punch.

Does this now mean that my entire career is over? That my work-future is over? Because I had mental health issues, does this mean that nobody will ever employ me again? Despite them possibly feeling the same as I did, I am now ostracised from society because I was mentally unwell? WOW.

I guess this explains why I have not been able to find work. Sadly I am neither smart enough, or creative enough to start my own business. And even if I did think of some magical way to start a business, it means that I will never be able to do business, as people will stop dealing with me when they realise I've been in a mental hospital.

I feel like a leper. Ostracised. Unwanted. Unwelcome. A disgusting part of society who belongs in some cave away from the civilised people.

Damn. That sucks. That really hits me deep. I will never be able to work again, simply because I had some mental health issues which were a direct result from physical chronic pain, and me not feeling good enough – not worthy enough to be in society.

As if that is not ironic enough, I find out that it is true – I am no longer worthy of being in society. Because I had a mental health problem, I am no longer worthy of being in society.

Damn

FUNNY STORY ABOUT AN ACQUAINTANCE

A ... "friend" I once had was an absolute jerk. A fairly short chap, whom I pitied. We frequently visited with them as it was a larger friendship circle in Cape Town where we had just moved to. I did not feel superior to him in any way – I feel inferior to most people. Rather, I felt sorry for this guy, as it was clear he had an enormously painful past. He tried to compensate for that by belittling others. I only saw him as a friendly acquaintance.

This "friend" once called me on the phone, and said "I won a trip to a luxury resort for myself and 100 of my closest friends. Will you please feed my dog when I am away?".

Of course, I was elated for him. I congratulated him, and asked him when I could pick up the keys for his house, so that I can feed the dog. I also asked that he writes down any treats etc I could get for his dog.

Then I heard laughter. Turns out, he had 3 people in his car, and had me on speaker phone for the prank. See, the prank was to insinuate that I was not part of his 100 closest friends. But I never even thought of us as friends, so I was more excited about being able to feed his beautiful Siberian Husky.

The people in the car were laughing at him, because I so swiftly celebrated his "Win" and my keenness on feeding his dog was something he didn't even think would happen. Like I say, I saw him as an angry little dog trying to bark at the lone wolf who had no care or quarrel with this pitiful little thing. If anything, I felt deeply sorry for him

Hypocrisy

Hypocrisy;
Hallowed be thy name!
Let others do what they want
And for the same, put me to shame

Provide me a lifetime or judgement
For marginally overstepping the mark
Which others do with abandon
Yet judgement at me they bark

Give me the confusion
Whilst I try understand
Why I'm not allowed
What others do with abandon

Grant me serenity
To live in daily frustration
And utter confusion
And pay for their misdeeds
Time and time again a penalty

FRIENDSHIPS (29 June 2023)

"War! What is it good for?" - I love that song by Edwin Starr.
In a similar vein, I could sing "Friendship! What is it good for?"

Being autistic, I really do not grasp the importance humans place on Friendships. For a start, I do not know when a friendship starts. When I was 12, there was a boy I particularly enjoyed hanging out with. I loved him. Not romantically. I just really enjoyed his company. One day, I mustered the courage to write him a letter to ask if he'd be my *best friend*. I felt the need to qualify "Best Friend", as in my 11 year old mind, there was a hierarchy of friend.

It is a hierarchy I've still not been able to measure or understand.

I guess what I am trying to say here, is that I do not understand friendships.

I write about friendship, as last night I had to go meet someone from church for coffee. This ... "phase" of life I am in, I am not interested in friends. Rather, not interested in creating new friendships. I don't have very long to live anyway, so what is the point? I mean creating friendships takes time and really, I have so little energy to live at this point.

But this man *wanted* me to come visit. He doesn't have a car, so it's on me to drive the hour to him. Which is a big deal for me, as most days I feel unwell, or just not in the mood to do anything.

BESIDES, WHY WOULD ANYONE WANT TO BE FRIENDS WITH ME?? I would not want to be friends with me. Maybe they don't know what a failure and loser I am... Maybe I should point it out to them. "Don't be friends with Nico. He is a manipulative asshole". Maybe I'll make mugs that say that – hand them out to anyone who is stupid enough to want to be friends with me.

Anyway, so I drove to meet this man at Burger King. Begrudgingly. The first half hour or so was like pulling teeth – slow and painful. We made small talk, which I hate. General idle chit-chat that I have neither the time, nor strength for. Then we started delving into our shared experience as immigrants. Damn. Talk about taking a hard left turn!

He initially shared about the fact that he moved to the UK from [unspecified] country, but had to leave his 2 year old daughter behind. Which was a tough thing to hear (and for him to do).

Then he shared the truly gut-wrenching story – his first wife committed suicide after killing their 8 month old daughter. He got home from work to see his daughter's lifeless body floating in the sea. Despite rushing her to the hospital, she had been dead for hours. Then he went home – only to now find his wife's lifeless body in the surf as well.

How the hell does a person step back from that? How do you pick yourself up, and carry on with life? A spouse I can understand. But an 8 month old baby with her whole life ahead of her?

As he told the story, salt-soaked water welled in my eyes. I looked at this poor man, who has this very recent heartbreak – heartbreak isn't strong enough... Heart devastation?

I told him of my suicide attempt, and we spoke about his guilt, feeling he should have been able to help his wife. I told him to stop feeling guilty. I don't think anyone can help pull anyone else from the brink if they are truly on the brink. But I also have a great deal of empathy for his poor wife. I've been in that dark place where I've stared Death in the face. Where I tried to run towards Death. Whilst I was not successful, his wife was. I think maybe it helped that I spoke candidly about my own experience. That he knew what my "last thoughts" were – that they were not of malice, but love for my family. That ending my life was a "gift" to my loved ones, so that they would not need to put up with me anymore.

I cannot speak for others really. People are so enormously complex. And suicide is such an enormously complex issue.

So there we sat, forming a friendship over shared frustration as immigrants, joy shared over finding each other and being able to visit, and some solace in shared, open, candid thoughts.

I drove to meet him earlier that evening, begrudging every mile. But I drove home after spending time with him, glad that I did so. A bittersweet evening.

EMPATHS (2 July 2023)

I once worked at a company with a particularly bright Data Scientist. She was great at her job, I suspect she was Neurodiverse (in some way), and the general field she worked in, quite straightforward. No nonsense. She didn't like putting on pretences. But she was also incredibly empathetic towards others. Of course, nobody really saw her as being empathetic. They saw her as cold and factual (which is no bad thing).

Interestingly, she was also often ridiculed and teased for "not being empathetic", which hurt her a lot.

The ironies abound; Those who accused her of not being empathetic, were in turn not empathetic towards her at all!

But, she was actually very empathetic. *Very much so.* She had a keenness and quickness in how she noticed others aren't feeling great. And she was great at meeting their needs in the moment; From helping them do a task at work, to making them tea or buying biscuits. Just something to alleviate their distress.

A senior leader even bought her a book once on "How people work", or some such – as a mockery of her apparent lack of empathy. But she understood people better, and more deeply than any of them realised. Of course, as an outsider, I noticed this and studied those interactions.

My point here, is that people don't understand empathy, especially as it pertains to Neurodiversity like Autism. People with Autism are often said to be cold and factual, uncaring even. But nothing can be further from the truth – at least as far as my own perception of the Human Race. I think people with Autism have a different type of empathy.

Which leads me to the concept of Empaths;

People often *think* they are "Empaths". Empath, as in; People with a higher than normal sense of empathy. The term Empath is generally met with scorn – indeed, my own views allude to my disbelief in how people seem to think they are Empaths.

But I think there is something to this phenomenon of being an Empath. Maybe it's not that even – call it "Telepathy" or "Precognition", whatever. Maybe it's just how normal people operate and because I am dense, I think it's some magical thing?

I have, at various times in my life .... "sensed" a situation is a certain way. When I then looked into it, the obvious data suggested that the situation in question is not what I sensed it to be. But most of the time, 90%+ of the time, I was vindicated in my belief that the situation was indeed what I thought it was – despite people claiming otherwise. There are numerous examples I can list of this. But these are mostly very, very sensitive and I'd rather not. But it is an interesting reflection on how I am often correct, despite not understanding people (or rather their motivations).

People have often ridiculed me for not understanding humans. Heck, I've ridiculed myself for not understanding people. Mercilessly. I tend to blame that on the fact that I have autism. I can understand the complexities of an internal combustion engine better than how people act. I once told a friend of mine that I prefer writing computer code for exactly this reason. In a computer, you can write a piece of code to perform a task. You can then count on the fact that the computer will execute the same code tomorrow, the day after, next week into perpetuity in an accurate, reliable way.

But people are different. You can say something now and it's fine, and tomorrow say the exact same thing, and you get into trouble. There's a ruleset at play that I do not understand.

YET! I am quite deeply empathetic. I have the ability to look *into* people, and perceive things about them, regardless of them admitting it or not. I am naive of course, so people can tell me an outright lie, for example that the clouds are made from gold – and I would believe them. Because why would people lie? And I cannot read between the lines either. But I am able to "sense" things with a part of me that my conscious brain cannot.

There's a particularly hurtful set of things that I have suspected for some time now.

Let's call it "Clouds are grey" and grant everyone involved a level of anonymity, including myself. So for some time now, a long time, I have suspected that "Clouds are grey". It's been pretty awful really. Suspecting this, but not knowing. Thinking I am the crazy one for thinking this. And yet, I've had confirmation that this situation is indeed as I thought. Not just that, but in fact significantly worse.

I am honestly a bit floored by this. I hope my future self has forgotten what the meaning behind the "Grey clouds" is, and lives on in bliss. (*May 2024: Yeah, sorry mate, I have no clue what you're on about?!*)

This chapter is rather just there as a confirmation for me that I am not as daft, and dim as I think and as people think. I am in fact a lot sharper in my perception of others. I am a lot sharper in knowing long before it is uttered, that a problem exists.

Another great example, is how a few years ago at work, I suspected something is wrong. My manager would lie to my face every time and tell me all is well. But I could sense it. It ended badly. I then went so far as to buy a quite grim-looking scorpion in amber. I have it on my desk as a constant reminder to not trust people, like the story of the Scorpion and the Fox;

How the Scorpion wanted to cross a river and asked a Fox to carry it across. The Fox refused, saying that the Scorpion would surely sting it. But the Scorpion promised it would not, so the Fox carried it across the water. Near the other bank, the Scorpion suddenly stung the Fox. As the Fox died and started drowning, it asked the Scorpion "WHY?". To which the Scorpion simply replied that it is in its nature.

That's really the situation. People promising they won't sting, and I naively trust them. But boy, they sting. Still, I choose to trust people. Naively so. And it's something I've taken flak for – for being so trusting. And often, I try take steps to alleviate the issue. But since I paradoxically also struggle to "read the room", the corrective measures I take are the wrong ones.

So I end up getting stung anyway. It's not fun to be honest. It downright sucks. For you to suspect a situation is a certain way, only to be sworn that it is not... and then later to find out you were right on the money.

So for now, whilst I was told and led to believe that the clouds are not grey, they are grey. Very dark grey. Ominously grey. And that's just from the little bit I know... The reality might be a lot worse. Which you know, is pretty damn awful.

GREY CLOUDS

Grey clouds gather on the horizon
Barometric pressure falls
A sure sign that the storm is coming

Yet, *they* say that there is no storm
They say that it's my imagination
They toe the line and pretend

No need to be alarmed, *They* say
It's a perfectly calm day
Prepare for a flood? No way...

They tell me I am paranoid
They lie to protect their vaunted morality
They tell me I am the fool who imagines the clouds

LIGHTING!
THUNDER!
Hail pounds the earth

Rain falls violently

Flood waters rise
Flood waters race
Water covers the world

You FOOL! *They* Say
How did you not prepare today
Now the waters have flooded the way

Yet when I asked, all was fine.
You knew the skies clouds were grey.
You knew the storm was rolling.
When I warned the village, you poured scorn on me
Vilified me for warning others of the danger

When I tried to be a lighthouse
You tore me down
When I tried to ring a warning bell
You threw the bell in the well
And cursed me for trying to stop further harm

Now at once I am drowning
Whilst you sit there frowning
And you tell me to stop clowning
You judge me for not being in the boat
You insisted there's no need to float
And now that I am drowning, you sit and gloat

In the maelstrom of the storm
Others have now been damaged
Some irreparably – innocents who need not have drowned
Yet I was the villain

Yet you knew all along
You made your heart a murder pit
And when I got up to fix, told me to sit
Now others have drowned
Lives destroyed by the damage
Yet you dismissed truthful warnings
You and others – and made me the focus of your anger

With my last gasps of air I try swim
When time and time again you lied on a whim

Yet now that I drown
You scorn with a frown
I am stuck with your boots of lead
My last gasp of air leaves me dead

Precipice

Again, I stand at the Precipice
Again, I pay for the sins of the father
Again, I pay for the sins of the son
Again, the burden is on me

Again, I stand at the precipice
Again, I am the one in the wrong
Again, no consideration for yourself
Again, you do not take some responsibility
Again, you do not apologise

Again, it is my fault
Again, the finger points at me
Again, the burden of sacrifice is on me
Again, the burden of sacrifice is on me…

Again, you stand with the dagger in my heart
Again, you point at your chipped shoulder
Again, you do not recognise your part
Again, you secretly twist the dagger in my heart

Again, you say I am the villain
Again, you lament your own sorrows
Again, you conveniently look past my pain
Again, I look for salvation under the wheels of the train

And that is how you will remember me;
Always the one in the wrong
You will never remember the pain you inflicted
You will never acknowledge the pain you still inflict

Whilst I try again to clean up my act
You will not see the hurt you caused as a fact
And all the things I legitimately worried about
Things you so easily lied about;
I know now are an empirical fact

Again, you say I am the villain
Again, you lament your own sorrows
Again, you conveniently look past my pain
Again, I look for salvation under the wheels of the train

Again, I stand at the Precipice
When I last stood here, I had no courage
Again I stand at the Precipice
But this time I have the courage

This time I jump
With the dagger still in my heart
To free you from my supposed villainy
Whilst you refuse to acknowledge your part
In every relationship it's always others' fault
Whilst you refuse to acknowledge your part

The Hurricane

Weak house!
Pathetic dolphin!
Useless boat!
Stupid human!

The walls of the house collapsed
Once protecting its occupants -
Suddenly washed away by the flood
The Hurricane asked in the maelstrom;
"Why weren't you stronger where you stood?"

Confusion filled the dolphin
Swimming in the ocean -
Suddenly yeeted into the sky
The Hurricane asked in the tempest;
"Why can you not fly?"

Engulfed by titanic waves
Sailing majestically across the ocean -
Against monstrous waves, naught but a mote
The Hurricane asked in the cataclysm;
"Why could you not just float?"

Horror filled the human
All around catastrophe and disaster
Lost in the Eye of the Storm
The human looked up and asked;
"Why cause all the destruction?"

The I of the storm...
Innocent is Me
I caused none of it
It's the fault of all those around
Little does the Hurricane see
It caused all the disaster to those who mourn

Little do we see that we're the Eye
We're the I
The I who causes the storm
The I who blames everyone else
We don't use our Eye to see the I
The endless disasters that in our wakes lie

BIRTHDAY (3 July)

Monday 3 July. I was born on a Monday. Tomorrow is my birthday, a day I used to look forward to. A day, all my childhood life, of a bit of acknowledgement and being treated.

All my adult life, I'd put in a day's leave, and enjoy the day. A profound feeling of peace, and in some way, accomplishment.

But this year, I am dreading the day. I am dreading tomorrow. There is, at time of writing, less than 10 hours left before midnight. Then I turn 45. I never meant to make it this far. I didn't want to live this long.

And yet, here I am. Darkening people's doorways. Afflicting the world around me with my presence

Presently, I am beset by the opposing desires in me;
On one hand, I just want to die. I want to sleep and never wake up. That would be so, so good.
On the other hand, I am actually feeling a little bit hopeful for the future. It's been a long time since I felt any hope or optimism.

There's another job interview this week. Another chance to try convince someone to see value in me. I've been unemployed for 5 months, and been unwanted at work for even longer.

Maybe I get the job this time. Maybe this time, I get to be of some use.

But again, I am beset by the cruel, cold, hard facts. I am not wanted. I am "Surplus to Requirements". It's clear enough I am no longer valued. It is clear from the perspective of other people that I am naught but a burden. An awkward inconvenience. To be discarded like used toilet paper.

So whilst I feel optimistic, I also feel a heavy sense of dread. No matter the salvation of a job; I will never be useful or needed again.

And so I ask myself; Is it even worth trying? Is it not better to just give up?

Those who told me I have value, are the same ones who lied about so much else. How do I trust? What kind of future do I have?

The river of Time
Time flows around me like a raging river
A torrent of water
Flowing with a rage that makes me shiver

Yet I stand in the middle
Time's river flowing around me
Carrying the detritus of my life to the sea

In the river I stand
My feet digging into the sand
Time rushing over my hand

And as it all flows to the sea -
The detritus of my life and me
I face Time's end with glee

ACTUAL BIRTH DATE AND DAY (Monday 3 July 2023)

Well, fuck. Here I am. Still alive. Interesting side note; I was ~~mistakenly~~ born on a Monday, and today is a Monday.

Now that I think of it, it seems altogether proper that I die on the day of the week I was born...

I've made peace with the idea of dying. I've made peace with death.

I am at the BMW dealership in Llandudno today. All day. There's a recall on my car to fit some kind of thing for free, which reduces emissions from my car. But I also need the brakes done, and the rear tyres.

I've planned well for my trip home though. "Home" – home as in afterlife. I've worked out the perfect plan this time. The benefit here, is that I am nowhere near home or near where it would traumatise my family knowing I was in this bush or the other. Out here, I have the freedom to pick a spot.

It's raining hard. It's about 13 degrees C outside, it'll help shut down body functions.

My plan is this – to use constructive waveform interference;

> **1 year later**, [Redacted] – I removed what was a carefully considered and calculated plan to help de-nature myself. This was written in a moment of utter despair and deep crisis. What I do not need, is someone else using the method and plan I created, and be successful. There is general guidance on writing mental health books which strictly prohibit (or strongly discourage at least) writing down any actual plan.

> Suffice to say that I am/was at time of writing in a dark place in life. Though it is now a year on, and I did not want to remove anything from the book, I did think it's best to revise this part at the very least. If not for myself, then at the minimum to safeguard others. I do not need blood on my hands

I WISH I HAD A GUN. I could put it to my head and it'd be an instant end. Not this stupid faffing with trying to calculate stupid formulas and coming up with clever plans etc. Pain in the arse.

I have a job interview tomorrow (Tuesday 4 July). Maybe a 2nd chance at redemption... If not... Well, I think there's only so much a spirit can take, you know?

IT'S SO EASY

It's so easy to judge
It's so easy to advise
It's so easy to encourage
It's so easy to find fault

BUT

It's not been so easy to walk these shoes
It's not been so easy to hear the same advice
It's not been so easy to feel discouraged
It's not been so easy to hear how I've failed

It's so easy to write your diary
It's so easy to write secretive thoughts about me
It's so easy to discuss me with others
It's so easy to agree about my supposed addiction

BUT

Where were you at 4am when I broke a tooth from gritting in pain?
Where were you when I've tried all the advice that doesn't work?
Where were you when my every neuron fires in agony?
Where were you when all I have is medication?

It's so easy to demand I change
It's so easy to demand I just look up
It's so easy to insist I think positive thoughts
It's so easy to write me off

BUT

You clearly don't know the cost of the slightest change
You clearly don't know how much I look up
You clearly don't know the price of positive thoughts
You clearly don't feel the pain of being written off

Please, just stop

POST BIRTHDAY BLUES

Well, the birthday came and went. I heard a quote online where someone said "You can always kill yourself *tomorrow*". It is slightly laughable, I know. But it has stayed my hand a bit. Though I am still convinced I need to exit the planet.

My wife has given up her psychology studies, which was part of the reason for me to write this tripe in the first place. As source material. Now I just… write. Dunno why really.

Maybe this helps others see the distress and darkness a person goes through before suicide? Maybe it'll help understand some of the complexity of the thoughts and considerations that goes into making this decision. Ending your life. It's no small thing.

Many people *think* they understand depression and suicide. Depressed people often would *think of* suicide. But it is more of a construct – like "World Peace". Or "Reducing Carbon Footprint". It sounds like a chunk of something you can chew on and understand. You think you have a hand on it. *But where, and how do you start?* How do you go about achieving World Peace? How do you start reducing carbon footprint – in the real world? How would you go about committing suicide?

It's much more complex than you think. Trust me, I did the research. I tried. I failed. You'd be surprised how often people attempt suicide...and then wake up the next morning, bewildered and confused. I did. I woke up bewildered and confused. Having taken actions and taking steps I cannot recall, no matter how hard I try! It does my head in.

But I want you to understand this;
For the most part, people like me who choose to (and try) end their lives first go through a very dark time. You might get frustrated. This person you know and love, is suddenly walking around with a sense of hopelessness.

I get it. I've been living this life for months. Trying to survive, but planning to end your life. I could have learned new computer code, or learned to speak Latin. Maybe spent time looking through astronomy data to see what cool things I could see.

I could have done pushups, I could have walked more, I could have done a hundred things.

But all I have been thinking, is *When is a good time to die?*. Planning, thinking about it. It's hard to think about long-term improvements in life, when you are actively planning on ending your life. When all your energy is focused on that one purpose, it is hard to think of how to improve.

When your energy has hit the floor, and getting up in the morning requires more energy than you have to just sit upright in bed. When all you want to do is die. When you cry yourself to sleep and your final prayer before you lose consciousness, is for God to end your life.

Then you wake up in the morning. The fresh horror of another day of failure. Failure on so many fronts. Rejection from so many fronts.

The darkness surrounds you. It's like a thick, black duvet that envelops you, and strangles you. For weeks – months, no, years, I have had this dark duvet around my head. Around my chest.

I have gradually gone from "Wanting to go to Dignitas to end my life", to actively planning my death. Even a place, and time. Exact sequence of medication to take, other methods at the same time as backups to ensure you die. The duvet gets thicker. The duvet stifles you. It sucks life from you. Even taking a single step is heavy – shoes like they're filled with lead.

Ending your life is no light decision. It's nothing that a coward does. Now that I have been through it twice, I know, it is not easy. It is in fact very hard. Much, much harder than you may guess!

If someone close to you ended their life, BE KIND. Understand that most people do not want to die. But given the options, that appeared to be the only option.

Just love them. Think of the loved one in kindness. They *did not leave you*. That is selfish of YOU to think.

The correct way to think, is that they became so overwhelmed with Life, that they could not figure out any other way to live. They – like me – probably thought that their death does you a favour. They – like me – might well see themselves as an obstacle. As a burden. So they acted to remove that burden.

As hard as it is to understand – and trust me, I am at this very moment I am writing this, thinking of alternative ways to end my life; Those who ended their lives likely did it out of LOVE for you. LOVE. They cared about you so much, that they decided to end their lives to save you from any further bondage or issues due to their continued existence.

Try see it as that. Try see it as love.

Or at least, see Suicide like this; Some sick people die from Cancer. Some sick people die from Lung Infection. Some sick people die from mental health (Suicide). It is tragic. But when working through your grief, think kindly about those who ended their lives.

In the thoughts I chronicled in this very-much-not-a-book, I hoped to explain something of my mental state of mind and despair in the days/months leading up to my death (if I die). My hope is that it helps YOU in YOUR journey to find acceptance and healing

SUICIDE IS NOT THAT EASY
I know exactly where
I know the exact map coordinates
I have all the tools I need
In order to end my life

But it's not that easy
I woke up after
Emotionally and physically scarred and bruised
And zero recollection of the event
But I know I tried
And I failed

Thinking about suicide is one thing
Fantasising about it is another
But when you have planned to the minute
In every minutia of detail how your life would end
Taking that last step is hard

Planning every action
Calculating the sequence
Then working on Plan B
You're literally working on how to end your life

And whilst I plan;
Did I try hard enough at Life, I ask?
Is there Hope that will arrive a day away?
Would I miss salvation by a week if I went through today?

"You can always commit suicide tomorrow" –
A useful quote I learned
It's a good way to step back and think about tomorrow
Maybe tomorrow will bring new hope
Hope...

Maybe there is some Hope still
Maybe there is some way out still

Maybe there is a way to win still
Maybe for now, I will wait until tomorrow

IN THE FINAL ANALYSIS (mid-May 2023)

Depending on how things go over the next week or two, this little writing exercise might end a bit abruptly – *if you take my meaning.*

I used to love peaches.

Especially the pits, the seeds. I loved gently chewing them, getting every last bit of the delicious peach off. It was as one might say, a thoroughly chewed bone. It's a nice illustration for my mental efforts to come to grips with my life ~~existence~~ as it currently stands (1 May 2023, 18:24). I have chewed this pit/bone about suicide quite thoroughly. Every crevice of it I explored to see if I can come up with an alternate. Probably like most people who decide on ~~suicide~~ *self-mercy*, it's at not at all a decision one ends up at casually. I can bloody well tell you that for free.

Getting the obvious out the way; I had a fairly OK day. Woke up in a daze and realised I am in the mental hospital. I was invited to go to the pottery class, which was thoroughly enjoyable. The hospital forgot to make my cheese sandwich, which I accepted as a sign to withdraw to my room. Tried to sit outside in the sun a bit – but I had neither the "leave" to do so, nor was I wanting to sit in the over-subscribed, smoke-filled quad. So one of the staff took me to the Occupational Therapy garden which was lovely.

But at some point, my back played up and the pain worsened. I'd hoped the pottery class and garden would help stretch my muscles a bit.

But over the last 4 or so hours, I've been reminded in exquisite agony *why* I am in this place. I am in this place because **I simply cannot cope with the pain any longer**. Physical pain. Emotional pain. Being unwanted, undesired and unwelcome. Just cannot anymore.

Wednesday is the big day for my job interview. I think if I don't get that, I am going to switch off this little Light Bulb. Might be a 2nd stage interview etc, and I will plan and prepare for it. But I think that is my Go/No-Go marker – which the psychiatrist is well aware of. I told him as much, which is why he punished me and detained me here.

But the last laugh will certainly be mine. They think we have each other over the same barrel, but I guarantee you that it merely seems that way ☺. From the energy drink's aluminium pull-tab which I hastily picked off in a panic at the Crisis Centre (in order to slit wrists), to my frankly genius Final Solution, I am ready.

Yeah.

Yeah I think I am.

Not sure my spirit can take much more crushing. Don't get the job, give people the gift of my departure.

Surprisingly many people have sent me lovely messages of support, encouragement and how much I improved their lives. But one has to wonder how many of those were sincere, and how many of those were just out of societal guilt.

But anyway, I am ready.

One big thing – MASSIVE thing – that has stayed my hand up to now, has been location. I didn't want to *desecrate* an area my family frequents, nor did I want to involve my car. This though, this location – hell, it's pretty far out the way. I can reasonably easily draw the line here, and it won't be a place they ever go near. Plus the staff are kinda trained for this eventuality. I've been quite consistently clear to all psych-whatever-ists that I don't want to traumatise first responders with a messy corpse. I've also made some effort to lose weight, so they would not need to handle an overly heavy corpse. There's still a lot of weight to lose. Lost 30kg since 1 October last year.

But as we're potentially so close to Day 0, there's not much more I can do. Sorry First Responders.

So there it is.

If the words on the pages suddenly stopped, that's why. Not going to leave suicide notes either – they rarely (from what I read) do anything more than create more questions, create more pain. For me, this whole thing has really been as a result of never-ending pain, which I am no longer willing to exist with. The job is just the catalyst – an opportunity to feel worthy as explained in chapter whatever.

Think what you will of those who commit suicide.

But I tell you these last hours are some of the darkest, loneliest, scariest times I've ever experienced. **Anyone suggesting that it is selfish or cowardly is a <u>fucking asshole</u>, and has no idea what they yap about.** Wait until YOU stand in the valley of Death, facing Death itself and see if you don't piss your pants.

On balance, I hope I've left the world a slightly better place than I found it. I have spent a lot of money and energy to help others. If that helped just one person, if just one out of eight billion can say "*Nico made my life even just marginally easier*", then I'd consider it a life well-lived.

Be at peace

TOMORROW IS A GOOD DAY TO DIE (25 July)

The Klingons in Star Trek have a saying "Today is a good day to die". Basically a (misguided) way to inspire warriors to fight to the death for honour. But I heard someone recently say that "You can always commit suicide tomorrow", which I liked. I'd be such a bad Klingon – preferring to die tomorrow!

Also, it is a rather idiotic way to communicate to people that they should retain a sense of hope, because things might unexpectedly get better today. So don't rush to end your life, you can always do it tomorrow.

It's a bit like people saying their diet starts on Monday, so over the weekend they eat 3 horses and 5 cakes. You suspend the bad, in order to enjoy a last bit of something nice.

It is ironically quite helpful to think that you "can always commit suicide tomorrow". After all, it is a pretty final solution, so if there are any other possibilities, exhaust those first, you know?

It's a weird concept, I know. But if you are in so much despair, at the edge of the precipice, it is a helpful thing to bear in mind. It is strangely empowering, even comforting.

I certainly cannot speak for everyone, so this is really just my own reflection. The idea that I don't have to rush to end my life is very comforting. We so often stress and anguish over things that might go wrong in future. Your car might break down, or your house roof might leak. Worse, you could lose your job, have romantic heartbreak etc. For many people, those scenarios might be "The end of the world". A rather dramatic view, as these things are survivable. People rarely *actually* mean that they'd die if they lose a job for example.

For me, I still lie awake at night – like last night – from immense back pain. Around 4am, I finally took a shot of morphine, and burnt my back with an excessively-hot hot water bottle. The pain never ends. Unless I die, that is.

Not that I am trying to play "Top Trumps" with suffering. Someone who has had a different life might genuinely believe their world is ending if they lose a beloved job, or a relationship ends. We each experience suffering to the extent that we know. For one person, an "Easy day" might be impossible to endure for another. Nobody should ever try and "win" a suffering comparison, as we each suffer in our own ways.

But with the pain that I cannot escape for example, Morphine to numb the pain and get a couple of hours of sleep is a better solution to dying. It's easy to say that now, being relatively numbed from my recent dose of morphine. But it is true.

People who actually love someone who is in mental distress might well prefer they had morphine instead of dying.

In many ways, the idea of "I can always commit suicide tomorrow", is a very empowering thought. Things have, objectively, not improved since I was in hospital. In fact, I learned some things that very much confirmed my suspicions I've had on certain issues before- and during my hospital stay. My reasons for wanting to end my life have definitely become even stronger.

Yet, after surviving my most recent suicide attempt, I decided that I can always commit suicide the next day. That alone, has given me so much peace. It sounds weird, I know. But it has. It's given me immense peace. I've made peace with Death. I've made peace in my heart with the idea of suicide, especially having a very good plan.

What this has done, is give me a "safety net". I feel quite liberated now. The worst that can happen, is I can die. Whereas I previously worried and stressed myself out over trivial bullshit, I now know that I have the freedom and power to end my life *when I choose*. So being fired for example, or whatever else would normally keep me awake at night have become reasonably trivial things. It's not that I don't care anymore. But I have peace knowing that I have a solution in case things go sideways.

Don't get me wrong! I am not advocating to anyone, at all, that suicide *should* be an option. Don't be stupid and think I am suggesting that. I am in fact un-suggesting that.

IN A PERFECT WORLD, NOBODY SHOULD EVER CONSIDER ENDING THEIR OWN LIFE!

This is merely my own reflection on my own situation. And I am really just saying that FOR ME, for MY OWN peace, I find solace in the idea that I can always end my own life at a later date. In my mind, that takes power away from other people who plan to betray me, or hurt me in any way. In my mind, that has given me a sense of peaceful surrender, knowing I have the power. Not other people

Perhaps though, this is something helpful for someone else. The fact that you don't need to rush to end your life today. You can always do it tomorrow. Or the day after, or Monday next week. Live, for as long as you have life, and can bear it. Who knows, there might be a very pleasant unexpected change in the near future that helps you get out of the deep distress you're in. And if not? Well, tomorrow is always an option...

THE DAY AFTER I DIE

After I die
Don't then stand at the coffin and cry
Don't then stand there and question why
For now, it's far too late now to try
Please don't stand there and cry

I'll never again smell the flowers
Or take immense joy in rain showers
I'll never again feel my cat's soft fur
Or feel the warmth on my lap of the mangy cur

Reserve your judgement and be glad
That you have never been in a place so bad
Where ending your life
Was your only option
Where you sat in the room with Death
And felt on your skin his icy breath

My death is your release
Your licence to do as you please
Without me being the millstone around your neck

The time is now right
For me to lose the fight
And go gentle into that good night.

The day after I died (19 July 2023)

After even more planning and consideration, I decided that Wednesday 12 July 2023 was now my last day on Earth. I recall the day with a vivid mixture of clarity and brain fog. I had been in a pretty dark place, and just could not go on anymore.

The nights leading up to it, I experimented with my various methods and settled on a way to end my life. I couldn't sleep for nights and nights. Frankly, I cannot remember when last I had more than about 4 or so hours of sleep.

On the day, I walked like my feet were filled with lead. I could not look my family or pets in the eye. I felt like a traitor. Yet, I had decided that my time had run out. That was to be the end.

At 5pm, I went for a walk with my wife, her cat and the dog. My feet felt heavy. Like lead. I struggled to lift my feet. Death, I knew, was here. My final day had dawned. I could not walk. It felt like I was swimming through mud. I had zero hope for a future where anything would improve at all, and knew that I needed to end my existence of uselessness and being a burden to absolutely everyone who knew my name.

We watched a BBQ Challenge show on Netflix. I looked at who the winner was by episode 2, as I was not going to live long enough to see it.

Around 21:45, my wife went to bed. I looked at my cat with a heavy heart as I gave her the night time "Lick-e-lix". I said goodnight to my wife, making sure that the last words I ever said to her were "I love you".

I dragged my leaded feet upstairs. Knowing that death was now only 3 hours away, I watched the last minutes of my life tick by. Firm in my resolution to end my life, I reminded myself one last time that it was the right course of action.

Choosing a final movie and a final meal was hard. We were on some diet, which I broke as I chose Buttered Popcorn as my last meal. *Top Gun Maverick* was to be the final movie I ever watched.

I watched the movie with intent. Determined to not waste my final hours on a stupid computer game.

Then I prayed. Like never before, in an attempt to gain forgiveness for what I needed to do. Interesting note that the Bible does not explicitly talk about suicide as an unforgivable thing. Ending your own life might not be a popular idea, but there's certainly nothing in the Bible that explicitly forbids it – despite what the Roman Catholic church might want you believe. In fact, there's only One unforgivable sin that is mentioned in Scripture, and I was not guilty of that.

I cried...

MAN UP! Fucking weakling.

Tears flowed. I reflected on my failure in Life.

Asking how it had come to this was pointless. Things were what they were, and I was not worthy of redemption.

Death breathed icy wind over my body.

I knew it was over.

I started my attempt. That took courage. Taking actual action to end it all. Never let anyone tell you that it is a coward's way. It takes a great deal of courage.

> May 2024 – a year later; Attempt details redacted for safety of others, and to avoid giving others ideas and inspiration. This "writing" was around my struggles in life and my own issues with mental health. It was not to serve as a way to help others end their lives. So in the interest of the safety of others, I chose to redact this part

I wrote a note to the Mental Health team – mostly so that they knew where to collect the corpse. No other suicide notes. Nobody needed my bullshit. Just GPS coordinates of where first responders can find the corpse.

I got my passport and driving licence out to have on me, so that the coroner can identify it.

Then I slipped into darkness...

The Dream;

The morning after I died, my wife woke up as normal. Fed the pets. Started work.

My sons woke up, went to work and studied, as normal.

The whole world went on, as normal, blissfully unaware that there was one fewer loser on the planet.

It was a beautiful day.

The sun shone as it had done for all of history. Fresh rain fell over the green Welsh hills – as if washing the filth of Nico away. At long last. My stench was gone. The world was free of me.

The funeral was a low-key event. My wife and two boys were at the crematorium. As stipulated in my will, I asked my wife to just chuck the ashes into the nearest rubbish bin, and forget that I ever darkened her door.

45 years, 9 days and six hours after I first cursed the Earth with my presence, my stench was finally gone. Done. Over with...

****

I had slipped into darkness the night before, in a state of deep crisis and despair. I don't know what happened. But at some point, I woke up. Surprised.
Appalled.
What a loser. Another suicide attempt failed.

What a loser. Cannot even kill myself properly! But I woke up, drenched in sweat.
Unbelievable.
OK, granted I didn't execute the entire plan as I planned. But still.

I then decided to not proceed. To not try again.

The next morning I told my wife. That was Thursday 13 July.

The day I ~~died~~ did not die.

Now I need to figure out what is next. But, I am looking at the future, imagining where it can go. Imagining possibilities and thinking about a life after failed suicide attempts.

There's little impetus from me to continue writing this *Not a Book*. Initially, it was meant to be a reflection on my stay in a mental hospital. Then it became a long piece of exposition about my broken mental health. But seeing as I am now past those events, I figure this is a good place to end this.

But I want to beg of you a few things;

Most importantly, if someone feels suicidal, *Just love them.* Do not preach to them. Do not share glib nonsense about "Having so much to live for" etc. Trust me, it doesn't help. In fact, it un-helps.

The human life force, and hope is so strong. Every instinctual drive in humans is to *live*. But more than that, to thrive and to have some element of peace in their lives.

You spouting clichéd nonsense, or "Encouraging" someone who is in such a dark place, is as helpful as an underwater hair dryer. Which is to say very, very unhelpful.

Know that a person who is suicidal – who even *admits it openly*, is in a deep state of crisis. Their thoughts are dark, they feel lonely and it is hard to think like a "healthy" person.

What you can do, is what Friend 2 and Friend 1 did for me; Just be there. Friend 2 wrote letters. Nothing profound. Just a hand-written letter to talk about her visit to Seattle, taking the dog for a walk, eating an ice cream on the beach etc. Not one single word of "encouragement" or other BS. In the darkness, it was so good to just get a hand-written letter from someone, with normal, every day content. A flicker of hope for a normal life in a dark ocean.

Friend 1 visited me in hospital, and outside of it. She never judged. Not once. Not once did she say I must feel better, or shake it off or anything of the sort. She just came to visit, without expectation or agenda, and was there for me. We laughed, we near-cried and sat in silence at times. Not once did she preach, or tell me that I need to get my butt in gear. That alone meant more to me than all the nonsensical, unwanted bible quotes and random videos without context that made me feel worse.

THAT is what you can do for people who are in crisis. Just go have a coffee. Laugh at a moth bumping into a window, or laugh at a joke that is less funny than it has right to be.

Being in a mental crisis where your every thought is bent on ending your life is not fun. It is a dreadful, heavy thing. So next time, look at suicidal people with mercy and grace. There may or may not be a reason they feel that low. But give them the space to breathe, and know that they are in a dark place. It is definitely not fun to be in that state. Then just love them. Just sit next to them. Be there if they want to talk, and if not, then silence is good.

But also know that if someone does end their life, it is not your fault.

If someone is so low and ending their own life is their *only viable* option for the future, then that is their issue. That decision is theirs and theirs alone. Do not beat yourself up about it.

Humans and their emotions are complex. My grandmother died from kidney failure. My father died from a heart attack. People die from illness sometimes. Mental illness is a real thing, and sometimes, people die from that. See it as that. See it as someone who was in such a tragic position, that they died from an incurable illness.

Then be kind to yourself. Be kind to the memory of those who ended their lives. They were in an awful situation and the decision to end life was an enormously difficult, heart-wrenching thing that required more courage than you will probably ever have.

So just be kind. Give yourself mercy and accept that not all illness can be cured.

Just be kind...

Journey's End

The sky fills with soft white light
Gentle tendrils of blue and gold
Reach all over like a loving embrace
A vision of the future
Filled with peace and grace

Colour and emotion collide
Inside my Synaesthestic mind

Gentle round tones sound like gold
Ting tung tung tung
Ting tung tung tung
Golden sounds in a cascade of white

Slender blue tendrils envelop
Left ear right ear
Left ear right ear
The tendrils ride forth like a heroic knight

Despite a lifetime of fear for the future
I now stand at the ultimate unknown
Enveloped by blue and gold
A life filled with fear and anxiety
Ends at least in peace and hope
I ascend into the mysterious darkness
In complete peace and blissful surrender

SINÉAD O'CONNOR

Poor Sinéad O'Connor! You know, I have been writing "Not a Book" for 2 months now (holy cow!). I think it is pretty obvious to anyone reading this that I have been relatively cavalier in regards to my own mental health. I could perhaps even be accused of simply not caring about my own mental health, and that would certainly be true.

But damn, other people... My heart breaks for other people. Whilst I see little value for my own life to continue, I feel so desperately sorry for other people who struggle with mental health. Take Sinéad who seemingly died by suicide this week (23 July 2023). Obviously she is a high profile figure, so her tragic death is quite a visible event. She's always struck me as a tortured soul, again one of those types of people I empathised with when I was in the mental hospital.

Someone who just strove for a small measure of peace.

I feel so sorry for her. Having attempted to end my own life, I know some of the pain that precedes an attempt. Not that I claim to understand how she (or anyone else really) felt, my own experience is that it is an immensely awful period. Again, speaking strictly from my own experience, Life isn't great all the time up to Monday, and then on Tuesday you make the decision to end your life. Situations deteriorate for a long time leading up to the decision. Sometimes, it is just your perception of events and things aren't truly that bad. Other times, objectively, things are really that bad – maybe even worse.

My point is that it takes a lot for things to be not great for a while, causing a person to experience such pain and suffering up to the point where they even make an attempt in the first place. That is the really awful side of suicide – people are often in crisis for a very prolonged period of time before they finally take the final action.

Mental Health advocacy groups have written a great deal on this topic, and people much smarter than myself have weighed in on all sides of the debate. Personally, I've been seen by a number of people over the last few months. From my GP, Mental Health nurses, Psychiatrists, Psychologists etc. It's definitely been my experience that many of those interactions have been ... I wouldn't say hostile, but definitely *less-than-friendly*. Take for example my first stay in the mental hospital. I went in, uncertain of what to expect. But it quickly became apparent that it was not a friendly, cuddly environment.

Whilst it was not cold and clinical, there was definitely an air of detachment and dare I say, "irritation" with myself and other patients. And I get it. We're all just human. Fallible humans. We each only have so much bandwidth to deal with

We did not ask to be born

HELLO OLD FRIEND! (27 September 2023)

Hello my old friend! No, not *you*, obviously. Chances are we've never actually even met. I mean hello to my Samsung S8 Ultra tablet, and bluetooth keyboard – and of course "*Not a Book*".

It has been a while since I wrote. 2 months in fact. Crikey.

Tempus has indeed *fugited*!

Tempus Fugit is Latin, which means "Time Flies". And by me needing to explain the "joke", you can now see for yourself why I am not often invited to parties. I am apparently not as funny as I thought. My doctor has often commented on my poorly developed sense of humour, and warned me to not use it on unsuspecting bystanders. Now you see why. In fact! My explanation, and subsequent apology for my poor sense of humour is often met with more raucous, sincere laughter than the actual joke. I wonder if I should become a stand up comedian who apologises to the audience after each joke. What a laugh would be had by all...

Anyway, 2 months since I last wrote. I am currently sitting at the dining table, looking out over the valley outside our the 203 year old chapel we live in, in rural Wales.

Not sure why I haven't written in so long. Maybe it is because I struggle with Object permanence – "Object permanence involves understanding that items and people still exist even when you can't see or hear them". I genuinely struggle with this to the extent that I am sometimes greatly surprised when my beloved cat walks into the house after she played outside. I love her. DEARLY. But when she's not inside where I can see her, or I don't think of her "*during dedicated cat thinking sessions*", I forget she exists...

Maybe because I've felt better? Interesting thought. I don't write when I feel OK. But I also don't write when I feel so very low. I kinda fall into the middle of the mental health gap when I feel just low enough to feel low, but not quite low enough to just want to sleep and disappear.

It's certainly not for want of content or events. In the last 2 months, both my sons have moved out and living on their own in opposite parts of the UK to where we live. Just one of them moving would have been a hell of a life event and adjustment to get used to. But both, just over a month apart... Damn. That's been quite a hit to take. I had children most of my life. We got married when I was 20, and had our first when I was 24. I am 45 now, so not quite half my life, but still, the boys were there for a significant part of life.

So to suddenly go from having 2 boys in the house, to suddenly none is quite a thing. I don't have the courage to openly admit how much I am struggling with this. Too much is the answer. I dare not even Google how to cope, because I cannot. I am struggling hard to cope. "Empty nester" is, I believe, the phrase used for people whose children move out.

It's strange you know? They're born and almost immediately, you become aware of how blisteringly fast time really flies. As an adult you're not quite aware how the hours, days and months go. But when you have children, you suddenly become aware. I recall when our oldest son first started primary school (I looked after them when they were younger, so never went to pre-school). The first school holiday was a welcome reprieve from the insanity of doing school runs and trying to organise life around school.

But the worst was the Sunday night before school resumed after the holiday. I recall staring out the window at the late winter's day sun with great sadness, thinking how quickly the holiday went by. There was so much I had wanted to do with the boys, then school started again. It's a perspective I never lost – throughout life I used to pause at micro events like this (weekends, short breaks etc), thinking how full of promise and adventure the time ahead seemed, and how quickly it went past.

I've often wondered if that is how people feel on their deathbed? You know, thinking back at life and how long a particularly stressful period seemed. Yet now that they are moments away from dying, how quickly life seemed to have flown.

Anyway, I am in that headspace now with the boys moving out. I am profoundly grateful that I *frequently* paused and made time to enjoy the moments. Enjoy the (sometimes awful) Christmas concerts, or whatever random events there were. Aware – very much painfully so – that those moments would end, and that one day I will be staring out a window on a rainy day, wishing I could have that time back.

Yet, despite enjoying the moments when we were in them, I cannot help but now rue the cold, harsh, unstoppable force that is the arrow of time. I miss my boys, despite them being grumpy old men now as well. 19 and 21. It feels like just 18 years ago that they were 1 and 3. In a way it is comforting that I knew, and mentally prepared for this moment. But the reality is that, despite "mentally preparing" as well as you can possibly try, no amount of preparation truly helps in the face of these massive life changes. Just got to ride each day out like stormy waves on the ocean, you know?

Life's Storms

You know the storm is coming
You see the dark clouds gather
You notice the barometer drop
You feel the hair on your neck stand up

You batten down the hatches
You lower the main sail
You raise the storm sail
You pack away the crockery

Mentally you are ready
Physically you are ready

Yet, when the storm lands it's all different
50 foot waves swell
Lightning splits the heavens, turning night to day
Thunder claps louder than a gun
Rain pummels your face, driven by a painful wind

You knew the storm was coming
You prepared as best you could

But now that it's here you fight for survival
Every threatening wave crests over your little ship
Every minute now a battle for survival
As gallons of sea water rush over and into your ship
Any minute now your boat can go under
Despite all your planning you are at the mercy of forces you cannot control

How easy it is to mentally steel ourselves for trouble
How insurmountable it can feel to try ride out Life's storms
How easy it is to think you are ready for the challenge
How tragically painful it is to live through the challenge to tell the tale

STILL LOOKING FOR WORK (27 September 2023)

Britain's beloved Queen near the end of 1992 referred to that year as "Annus Horribilis" – Horrible Year. I think for me 2023 qualifies as Annus Horribilis. Laid off early in the year, I think we were told around 6th of January, spent 6 weeks* (*so far...) in a mental hospital, unemployed, children moved out of the house, 2 suicide attempts, other things going, on and the worst is that October, November and December still lie ahead unfought. Like Sauron's army on the Pelennor Fields – vast forces still unfought. Damn, I don't even know if I have the strength to finish out September (I know, same old lamentation), let alone battle through 3 more months.

Those who are more ... superstitious(?)... often claim that good follows bad. I think it's just the law of averages, you know? Which I guess is a scientific mask for superstition, but it seems to follow logically that if a year was this shitty, then the next ones surely have to be a bit better.

One good thing; I discovered the band "Of Monsters and Men". I started listening to one of their songs towards the end of my last hospital visit. Actually the very one I am listening to as I write this – King and Lionheart. If I had one of the old cassette tapes with their music, it would have broken by now – that's how much I've been listening to them. A LOT. Don't know what it is about their music, but I find it quite comforting. Not all the songs though, I have about 5 or so that I listen to on repeat. I might listen to more in time, it's just that I like these 5 so much, I don't want to waste time listening to something else when I could be listening to something I actually enjoy.

I think if I survive this year, a lot of it will be down to "Of Monsters and Men" giving me some mental and aural peace in the middle of the tumultuous ocean of despair

So yeah, 8 months unemployed. My credit rating has gone to hell in a hand basket. I used to have a great credit rating 968 out of 999 at a stage. Then Covid happened and now it's mid 80s. Not like 980 or 800+, I mean as in around 84 out of 999. "Junk" or "Very poor", I believe Experian calls it. It is terrible. Needing to call the bank and various creditors to please and explain why I am in this dreadful financial situation.

Anyway, so looking for work – I reworked my CV yesterday. Not sure how much the effort is worth really. Feels like a study in futility. Earlier in *Not a Book*, I spoke – often spoke – of how useless I feel. Waking up every morning and going through every day with rejection letter after rejection letter really reinforces the idea that I have become useless. I mean, if I had any apparent utility in life anymore, I'd have had a job by now, you know? 500+ job applications, as many rejections.

So I reworked my CV. Astonishingly, there are people who say my old CV was perfect, just what the "client" needs. Then there are those who looked at the exact same CV and said it's crap. I had all beautiful data visualisations on, showing and highlighting how much money I've been worth to companies I've worked for. You know, succinctly highlighting every number so that within 10 seconds you had a great idea of what and how I've been doing. But no, apparently that is not good, and I had to redo the whole thing by writing endless walls of text. Made me a bit angry to be honest. I mean which hiring manager is going to read endless miles of pages of text? OK, I am being slightly facetious, but the point stands. I thought that a CV was just meant to highlight your key skills and accomplishments, so that the hiring manager is then interested in knowing more, then interviewing you and asking more pointed questions.

But OK, the introduction on my CV is slightly shorter than Homer's Iliad. Let's see how the responses pan out.

I just know I am tired of feeling like such a nil on a contract.

PIPPIN! Well, just PIP (28 September 2023)

If you were to ask a group of people what their most favourite scene in the Lord of the Rings movies is, I bet that a majority – maybe even you would agree which scene it is. Out of all 3 movies, original or extended versions, there is one scene that really is so profoundly epic, that you'd have to be an emotionless Vulcan to not be moved by it.

I am, of course, talking about the scene in Return of the King, where Rohan arrives on the Fields of Pelennor to break the siege of Gondor.

In the movies (slightly different in the books), the Witch-king of Angmar had just broken Gandalf's staff, the City of Minas Tirith seems lost and it seems that powerful though he might be, Gandalf is also about to die. Then you hear it. Feint at first, then louder. The camera cuts to a soldier from Rohan blasting on his horn, you get goosebumps and you see the mighty army of Rohan in the dawn's light, ready to bring destruction to the forces of darkness. It's an amazing scene to watch and listen to with a good surround sound system.

That moment of reprieve, that brief moment of light that shines into the darkness that helps you see that Night – the bad – won't last forever.

It's a scene that I've often thought of in life. Yes, the big fight is only now truly about to start, and thousands of noble, good, brave soldiers are now going to die. But it is an important reprieve from the overwhelming shadow and death that existed and lights a tiny flicker of Hope.

That is how I feel today.

After *months and months* of filling in paperwork, doing calls, going for embarrassing meetings, the UK Government agreed to provide me with Personal Independence Payments (PIP).

It's a small amount of money – from what I understand, between £26/week to £150/week. This is to help you gain a measure of *independence* if like me, you are struggling with back issues and cannot do things like tidying or cooking easily (and without needing to shore up with morphine for the inevitable pain).

Following the analogy, this morning the Department for Work and Pensions blew the horn on Gondor, by sending me a text to notify me that they have approved PIP for me. How much is anyone's guess though. I will only find out mid-October how much it is. Like I say, not a heck of a lot. But at this point, every little will help tremendously.

In the darkness of my year, there is at long last, a tiny glimmer of Hope.

And literally as I finished writing this chapter, a recruitment agent called me to arrange an interview with a company who really liked my original CV and want to discuss a job opening they have for Friday 29 September at 4pm. Perhaps this time, I will be victorious and able to push back the darkness to a new dawn of Hope and Life

They ended up granting me part of the PIP allowance, which helps enormously. I mean I truly struggle to make a meagre, unappetising hot dog and fries as the pain is just too great and my legs literally go numb.

I am so profoundly grateful for the help the PIP is granting me – a bit of room to breathe really!

The first tangible lifeline whilst I gasp for air as I drown in an ocean of despair

I WILL TAKE THE RING TO MORDOR...
(28 September 2023)
... Though I do not know the way

Another memorable quote from the Lord of the Rings movies. Frodo offering to do what must be done, though he has no idea how to do it, or where even to go.

So where to from here for me? Where is the Mordor that I carry my "ring" (mental health) to? Don't know really. But I cannot keep rambling on like this I guess.

My wife was surprised earlier today when she asked if I am *still* writing this. She thought I had finished. To be honest, I also thought I had finished. Ha! I mean, this stupid "book" has more "endings" than the Return of the King had.

On my way home from a GP appointment today, I did reflect on this though. I wondered when I would feel OK enough to finally click Save and Exit from this document. I figured it would be when I am "better". But I do not exactly know what "better" even means in this context.

I guess I am no longer using profanities to the level and frequency I did earlier in *Not a Book*. It's like an Orange. You want orange juice, you squeeze the orange and presto! Orange juice comes out. Not because it's magic or something, but it's because the orange is filled with juice and fibres, so obviously you expect orange juice to come out of the orange instead of chilli sauce.

Much the same with humans really.

You squeeze the human and what comes out is from what is inside to begin with. The fact that I seem (as far as it is on paper to be so), "lighter" and better, must mean I am a bit better than earlier in the year. I still have many, many moments in a day when I think humanity would be better off if my character were deleted from the *Life game*. I still think I would be completely OK with dying if the doctor told me tomorrow that I've run out of time.

Heck, I even still often wish I were locked up in the mental hospital again. For many reasons, but probably not the ones that appear obvious.

But I guess for now I am OK. Which is better than I have been. So that's "good", right? Surviving for now? Applying for jobs, trying to plan for the future. Feels better in my head at least.

I think ChatGPT will be relieved to be sure! Poor ChatGPT! Ugh, what a sentimental sucker I am, feeling sorry for an AI language robot.

I have been using Open AI's ChatGPT to review my writing, as I feel it to be a cruel ask for a healthy human to have to review this mess. In the Expanse TV show, there's a scene where Miller and Holden received lethal radiation poisoning. After a harrowing escape from a space station, they are taken care of by the automated medical facilities on the Rocinante. After recovering somewhat, Amos remarks that the ship's automated medical systems kept trying to switch to palliative care mode (meaning the machine is even giving up).

In the same way, ChatGPT kept trying to switch me to "palliative care" mode when reviewing my work. It kept telling me to seek – to urgently seek – professional help! Poor AI. I wonder how much of a learning experience this has been for ChatGPT?

Chat GPT, I don't know if you can understand this, but I am deeply sorry for the trauma I put you through by asking you to review this. Rest assured no other human could have

OK, LET'S LAND THIS PLANE... (mid-October 2023)

In answer to my wife's encouragement of finishing this up, I thought I'd raise a few points. Mostly points my wife made.

ChatGPT has been rather generous in its response and reviewing of my "work", saying that I "reflect a profound self-awareness". It has consistently credited me for being "Introspective". I am not sure about that. Being introspective seems that it should be more profound than – you know, *this* mess. Should be deep, moving, wise even in a way. All I am doing is typing what I am thinking. Maybe that is being introspective? Who knows even? I blame having autism for not understanding how these things work.

Anyway, so wrapping up;

I half incredulously asked my wife what she meant when she said I must wrap this up with things I have learned. I asked her for some examples of what she means, as I am not certain I learned anything from this year.

No wait, that's not correct.

I've learned to definitely not trust mental health professionals.

That's a big one. They punished me this year for feeling so deeply troubled and depressed by locking me up in a place I first had no business in being, but which I now ironically miss!

They stopped me from ending my life when I was feeling so low and pumped me full of drugs which on reflection only seemed to make things much worse. So definitely that is what I've learned; To not trust mental health professionals.

I guess that is unfair. To an outsider, the fact that I am still lingering like a particularly bad fart in an elevator is evidence that the mental health intervention "worked". But I contest that it would only have been the case that it worked if I had been a valuable person, or that my life had some purpose or contribution to the world – which it doesn't.

But further to my wife's points she raised;

"What did I learn this year?"
If you haven't learned anything from the year, it's been a waste...
Ha! Tell me about it. I touched on this concept a bit earlier in *Not a Book*, where I reflected on the fact that I only *existed* during my hospital incarceration. I waited out the time until they'd let me go and I had freedom to pick how I'd "Delete my Save Game". There was no profound learning, there was no profound introspection or discovery about myself. None was sought, none was found.

It was a waste yes.

Not sure what to add to that really? I am not sure – and no offence to anyone here – not sure how one expects a person who was in such a low dark place (and in many ways still is), to learn or to strive to be better. Learning, improving only really happens when you can imagine a future and want to do your future-self the favour of learning something so that the future-self has an easier life. I wanted to prevent June-Self, July-Self, September-Self from existing entirely. That's all.

I guess I did learn which suicide methods do not work. But I don't think that's something to admit, I mean I shouldn't admit which do not work... There is strong "guidance" on suicide and related methods on various anti-suicide websites, basically saying to not provide detail.

What did you learn about others?

Ah! This is interesting. I think I did learn something here. Inadvertently though. It's not like I was *studying* people. There was that one night that I was so annoyed with the one patient in hospital – the one who kept sobbing, wailing and crying. Sitting there in my self-righteous dickishness, I overheard one of the staff commenting that she is "singing" to comfort herself. I broke that night. My heart shattered into millions of pieces when I realised everyone just wants a measure of peace.

It's changed my outlook post-hospital quite dramatically. I generally consider people with a great deal more empathy now than I did pre-hospital. Realising that people all over, rich or poor whatever – people don't ask to be born. They're thrust into a cold, cruel world where empathy and understanding is scarce. They – we I guess – wander through life just trying to make sense of this bewildering chaos we're dumped into, and have to try figure things out without a manual or FAQ guide. Some are born into countries that are at war with neighbouring countries because of some dispute, others are born in countries where water might be scarce, others where it floods. Nobody gets to pick a "spawn point" before they arrive here. They're just unceremoniously dumped in an area and need to survive. We all really are just trying to find a small measure of peace.

THAT truly has been the biggest thing I learned this year.

Though I am probably still a massive arsehole to an outside observer, I do weep for humanity behind the scenes and feel a powerless rage and desire to want to help people. But I appreciate I am the last person in the world that anyone needs help from, so I will sit on my hands and stay out of the way.

What did you learn about yourself that wasn't there
Not sure really.

I have never considered me among the very intelligent or the very wise. All my inspiration from life have come from other great characters I admire, then try emulate that. Like Captain Picard or Commander Data – maybe Dexter from the TV show Dexter. You know, ordinary normal people who seem to have life figured out, seem to be pretty normal, stable people whose actions I can emulate and then not fail too badly at in life.

Heck, I have even taught my sons that if they are ever in a difficult situation in life, to think of how I would react – *and then do the complete opposite.*

So I am not sure what I learned about myself that wasn't there. Except maybe the empathy thing.

> **May 2024**: You ended up learning a crap load about yourself Old Boy! I hope you realise that. Especially in the next few chapters – you did a lot of discovery there. A lot of great stuff that brought you immense calm, peace and acceptance! The story really is not over until it is over…

How did you come to grips with not working? How have you found the strength to get up in the morning?
Guilt.

Guilt.

That's what "drives" me at the moment.

I still feel very depressed and struggle with my back pain and related issues a fair bit. Plus, not having a job is making me feel very embarrassed and useless, and frankly I do not have the courage to be awake and face the world every day. So all I want to do is sleep until my body hurts so much that sleep is uncomfortable, then go play games on my PC. But for whatever reason that is not socially acceptable.

But mostly, my wife is working hard and doing what she can to keep the boat afloat, so I try to get up and motivate myself to do things around the house; Make food, tidy etc to help her out.

Not sure what else to say – that is just the honest truth. Guilt drives me at the moment. I'd rather not follow this rabbit hole much deeper, as I know where it ends, and it is not a place I really want to be...

AH! WOW, look at that. Not wanting to follow the particular rabbit hole about my drive/lack thereof, highlights to me a thought that I might actually be doing better than earlier this year. Not wanting to return to the dark place that this particular hole leads to. That's an improvement, isn't it?

TEMET NOSCE – "KNOW THYSELF" (29 September 2023)

This is one of the most pithy, but also one of the most profound statements in life. It seems so obvious, but also so difficult to attain. Truly attain.

Over the past few months, I have spent a significant amount of time studying philosophy, learning about emotions, how the human brain works etc. It's a topic I've never bothered to delve into much, as I used to consider it "hokum". A statement not entirely without merit, as things like emotion cannot easily be measured, and I like measuring things. This much should be clear if you've read through this mess and recall for instance my yearning to measure what a friend is, or how much friendship is worth.

Take for example the diagnostic criteria for assessing ADHD. Even reading the acronym "ADHD" will instantly conjure up images of hyperactive *boys*, running amok in the classroom. It's something easily measured; How long someone can sit still and pay attention in a classroom environment.

ADHD – a bigger deal than people know

I bring up ADHD, because I think I have it. Well, ADD – the *Hyper* component is definitely not me. But ADHD is now the catch-all phrase that is used, with a focus on cases like mine being "inattentive". This took me a while to realise, as I have often in the past few years wondered if I have ADD(ADHD). Apparently though, the Hyper component of ADHD can also refer to one's thoughts, which are hyperactive and race around like a racehorse on *speed*, which my thoughts most definitely do.

My wife would roll her eyes and immediately say I have ADHD.

The mess and clutter from my litany of interests and hobbies in the house tell that tale all too well. Even trying to watch our regular

YouTube Trio of Canadians (Slim Potatohead, Foresty Forest and Steve Wallis) on a Saturday morning is fraught with distractibility. As I scroll down my Subscriptions list, there are new videos on Physics, or someone making a fun new diorama, putting LEDs into things that shouldn't have LEDs in – I mean it's a nightmare because I get distracted. So my wife often *drives* the remote to find the shows.

But my having ADHD was less obvious to me. In fact, I have even tried to do online assessments, which I never finished, as I'd get sidetracked by a thought and go down a different rabbit hole. Maybe the test asks if I prefer a black or blue sweater, and instead of answering the question, I'd think of how the number 5 is a blue colour, and Fridays are black. Also, does every galaxy in the universe contain a supermassive black hole – remembering the awesome "Supermassive black hole" song from the Twilight movies. Ironic as this might sound, I swear I wasn't going to write all that. I started thinking of an arbitrary example then my mind wandered…

Point is, it was only when I was assessed by one of the clinicians during my hospital visits, that they suggested I have ADHD.

One of the lesser-known facets of ADHD is "Emotional dysregulation". In fact! The DSM 4 (Diagnostic and Statistical Manual of Mental Disorders) guideline, which was only replaced in 2022, did not even contain any guidance on Emotional Dysregulation. If memory serves the new DSM 5 which includes Emotional Dysregulation, is considered "controversial" for including this.

Step back; What is Emotional Dysregulation? Basically, it is the ability to regulate/manage your own emotions. Silly example, let's say you bump your toe against a chair. A "normal" person who is able to adequately regulate their emotion will see this as an accident, deal with the pain, calm down, and move on with life.

But someone who struggles with Emotional Dysregulation would react quite differently. Instead of calming down, they might instead *calm up*, and curse. Then falls down the rabbit hole to first regretting the day they bought the chair, then getting angry at the sort of buffoon that would even make a chair with triangular feet that hurts cold, naked toes so much. Maybe then filling with rage, wishing you could find out this person's name and address, so that you can go burn their house down and stick a potato up their car's exhaust.

Like I said, silly example. But it is not far off from the kind of "adventures" my emotions go on when things happen. It's not just bad things either.

Emotional Dysregulation speaks to the general inability for some people to experience, manage and generally temper their emotions. Overreaction basically.

Why am I writing this wall of text? Well, Temet Nosce – it's something I've learned about myself.

All my life, I've struggled with how to act/react appropriately in awkward situations. As a child, my dad would just threaten me with harsh punishment for "sulking" or just straight up giving me hidings if I acted inappropriately. Not that I even knew what appropriate was in that situation. As my mind desperately raced to come up with some sort of reference on how to act, I'd outwardly shut down, upon which I'd be labelled as being "dikbek" (pouting/sulking). But it was only because I clenched my teeth due to stress, as my dad used to hit me so hard that I'd pee myself – which in itself I'd be punished for. So the threat of hidings were quite horrendous.

That trauma of not knowing how to act and respond has stayed with me all my life. The desperation that sets in when I realise I've done something "wrong" (despite how trivial) and then panicking and trying to desperately overcorrect. I remember when I was 7 years old, I accidentally dropped half my towel in the bath after I got out the bath. That was a "wrong thing". I tried wringing it out, but unfortunately I could not dry it.

How would a normal person react? It would be a non-event. After all, towels are designed to get wet!

How did I react? After a desperate panic from not being able to wring-dry the towel, I walked down *death row* to the living room to go tell my parents about the horrific, unforgivable thing I did, and to apologise as remorsefully as I could, just so I would not get a hiding!

It's pathetic. I know.

But it effectively illustrates the difficulty I've had in dealing with situations.

What is weird, is that I have Autism and ADHD together. The careful planning side of Autism sometimes clashes, and clashes hard with the impulsivity of ADD for example. It's interesting though that Autism and ADHD are apparently opposite sides of the scale, 50% - 70% of people on the Autism Spectrum also present with comorbid (relating conditions) ADHD.

Synaesthesia:

Even more intriguing, is that whilst only 2% - 4% of the general population has Synaesthesia, around 20% of people with Autism have Synaesthesia! Synaesthesia, if you are still unfamiliar with it, is a condition where you for example "hear colour", or "see music".

I actually have multiple forms of Synaesthesia;
1) Grapheme-Colour – Letters/Numbers are associated with certain colours
2) Chromesthesia – Sound/Music causes you to "see" colour. Or associating sounds with colours. You know those kaleidoscopes you had as a kid where you look into a tube and turn the thing to see different shapes/colours? That's kinda what hearing music does in my brain
3) Spatial Sequence – Seeing things/events/memories as points in space
4) Number form – Like a mental "map" that you experience with numbers in different locations
5) Ordinal Linguistic - Concepts such as numbers, day names, months etc are associated with personalities or genders. Like number **5** is **blue** Exactly #1520A6 / RGB: 21, 32, 166, and really the friendliest of all numbers. Number 2 is yellow, and is

like a cuddly teddy bear, where 3 is a hostile number, gloss black and wants to bite you.

Perhaps the worst though, is Misophonia, which is a "neurological disorder" which triggers very negative emotions as a result of certain sounds. There have been instances where I've been with a person eating a certain type of breakfast, making a certain kind of sound which drove me into such a rage, I'd have gladly dug their heart out with a teaspoon!

It's not clear that Misophonia is really Synaesthesia, but there was some research which suggests it is an auditory-emotion Synaesthesia. In fact, there's a study (https://www.ncbi.nlm.nih.gov/pmc/articles/PMC6964854/) which suggests that "Misophonia is associated with worse cognitive control when exposed to misophonia trigger sounds". The conclusion was that "Results from the present study provide evidence that misophonia may significantly deplete cognitive control when people with elevated misophonia symptomatology are placed in misophonia symptom-provocation circumstances" – meaning basically that Misophonia can severely affect your mental self control.

So in one brain, you have Autism, ADHD and Synaesthesia. All three these are documented to be physical differences in the way the brain functions and indeed, is constructed.

Is it any wonder then, that I struggle to fit into a societal norm, when my brain is so very, very … "weird"? The thing literally does not look like, or function like a normal person's brain?

I became aware that I had Synaesthesia about 10 years ago, when I learned to my great surprise that other people didn't see blue as 5. I mean 5 as blue. Or a Monday as red.

The Autism I've known about for 7 years now. Had I known sooner in my life that I had Autism, I might have been more kind to myself in the first place. But I might have also operated differently with people, and made very different choices which did not rely on my pretending that I am a "normal, well-adjusted" individual. I think if you've read this far in this absolute mess of *Not a Book*, you'd certainly agree that I am not exactly normal. Or well-adjusted.

But the ADHD is new, and it is interesting to me that these 3 neurological conditions are all present in my brain. I agree that (philosophically at least), this does not give me an "out" – an excuse – for my abhorrent behaviour and reasoning.

But as my attempts to go to know myself better, this is a good start at trying to understand and accept that I am not normal, and that is not wrong. I am not not normal because I am purposely trying to be a dick. I am not normal, because my bloody brain is literally a factory error, and the thing is physically faulty – wired incorrectly. It is not, as far as I know, anything that can be fixed with medication or surgery.

Although, if any neurosurgeons read this and think they can fix it, get in touch! I'd love to be fixed.

Except the Synaesthesia. That must stay. Synaesthesia is said to be a "Neurological condition" like it is a bad thing. But it has enriched my life in ways I cannot begin to explain, and I cannot imagine a life without it.

When my wife initially challenged me to think of what has changed, what I've learned in the past year, I was hard-pressed to think of something on the spot.

But as I tried to swim through the mud of my mental state this past year, and tried to read about topics ranging from psychology, to how the brain functions, I have come to learn that I should be more kind to myself.

It's not like I ever *chose* to be like I am.

I am a **Friday car**.

"Friday car" means basically that the factory workers have had a long week, and this is the last car they build on a Friday before the weekend. So with their minds more fixed on the weekend, they all do a careless, half-arsed job. So every damn component, hinge and wire is a poorly built- and fitted endeavour. There is not one thing you can do to fix it – the entire car is a poorly-built piece of junk, that was assembled badly.

And that is what I have realised I am – a Friday car.

On the face of the comparison, it might seem that I am being unkind to myself. But I find some solace in that. After a lifetime of trying to be normal, and failing miserably, the conclusion to my Annus Horribilis (horrible year) has brought me to a point of self-acceptance.

I can finally accept who I am, and love my broken self for who I am...

> **MAY 2024**: Little did I know when I wrote this, how much knowing I have ADHD would help me. The profundity of that knowledge is impossible to overstate.
>
> Even for myself, who is quite outspoken about Neurodiversity, it was a surprise at just how enormously ADHD impacts your life. This knowledge and how it impacts people has helped me understand myself better than I ever did. Just a pity it took so damn long

WHY IS AN ADHD AND AUTISM DIAGNOSIS IMPORTANT?

I'll tell you;

You go through life, always feeling like a failure and a social reject. You don't understand how or why people do things they do. You try mimicking their actions, and fail.

During an office party where everyone is chill and telling funny stories, you try fit in. You remember being told by your manager to be less awkward. "Get out of your shell a bit". Or "Be yourself". So you think everyone is having a good time, you will join the banter. You tell them about the VERY FUNNY shark attack in Cape Town, where a Great White Shark bit into a semi rigid inflatable (RIB) boat.

Everyone stares at you aghast and your manager tells you off for being an arsehole for telling such a distasteful story, despite nobody actually being hurt in said real event. I mean it is a funny video – look it up on YouTube. Apparently, I am a broken thing who does not even understand humour. Dumbass…

You then carry on through life, alone and lonely because you clearly don't know how to do friendship.

Then one Friday morning you lose your job - for which you consistently got EXCEEDING EXPECTATIONS reviews, brought in nearly $20m in business in just one year, rescued an entire team of 18's jobs, helped 3 people get a promotion and despite being bullied and abused by a certain Vice President, get her butt saved and promoted. But you lose your job, the only thing you actually understood and were good at.

Your life comes crashing down on you. You try commit suicide 3 times, you're locked up in a mental hospital for months and life just crashes and burns around you .

****** HOWEVER ******
~~Luckily for me~~ - I mean my friend! *Yeah, definitely not me...* Luckily for my "friend", you at long last by chance discover you're Autistic and have ADHD.

Overnight, your entire world view changes. With impact hammer force, EVERYTHING suddenly makes sense. Over the next few months, you start understanding why you cried more about Battlestar Galactica being destroyed, than any human character.

You understand why you prefer to write thousands of lines of code without talking to one single human.

You understand you have ADHD and that's why Caffeine makes you sleepy
You understand that you have ADHD, which is why you have a hundred different hobbies and half-finished passion projects.

And whilst you might be depressed, just the very fact that you now understand that you're not entirely a useless Friday Car - your brain is physically just structured differently to other people's!

Life just suddenly makes sense. In the blink of an eye (just about) your suicidal tendencies vanish in exchange for wanting to get to know the person you've spent 45 years with (you)

I HOPE PEOPLE GET DIAGNOSED EARLIER. IT MAKES LIFE SO MUCH EASIER

ALSO AS FAR AS I AM CONCERNED; Self-diagnosis is/should be very valid. A "normal" person won't go trying to find answers to why they feel like an alien on earth. People with ADHD and Autism struggle to fit in and understand the world around them, so they search for answers.

AUTISM: For Autistic people, they will have the obsession and diligence necessary to read through things like the DSM 5. They'll be able to, and capable of finding the DSM5 and reading/studying the 992 pages (May 2024) and find the answers. "Normal" people won't even know the DSM 5 exists. That alone should be evidence for Autism

ADHD: Well… ADHD. Inattentive or Hyperactive type. Neither of these two classifications would have the patience and desire to read a pretty dry document like the 992 page DSM 5 to try find answers for why they apparently don't fit in to the world. The mere fact that they would put themselves through reading / finding the DSM 5 alone should be enough to satisfy diagnostic criteria! Hell man, even just going through the torture of looking for, and doing a 50-question quiz to find out if you have ADHD should be sign enough that someone has ADHD. "Normal" people won't have trouble sitting through the 50 question quiz. Hell, they probably would not have searched for the quiz in the first place.

ADHD (in my mind) is a much more profound issue than "just" autism. I'm not trying to downplay autism here. I'm rather trying to point out (as I said earlier) that ADHD is not just a naughty boy who cannot sit still in class.

ADHD has a litany of profound impacts on a person's life. If you think trying to get/having an ADHD diagnosis is just trying to find a label or seeking attention, think again. In the first instance, stop being a judgemental arsehole about it. Then go read up about it.

Seriously.

If you judge people who have ADHD, go read about it and see how profoundly it can affect people – from all ages.

I cannot, *ABSOLUTELY CANNOT* overstate the moment, the gravity of the psychiatrist finally telling me I have ADHD. And then learning how utterly profound Autism, but ADHD especially affects people. ADHD is not just some cute little thing where boys can't sit still. It is such a colossal impact on people, in so many ways.

LANDING GEAR DOWN, FULL FLAPS
(28 September 2023)

In aeronautic vernacular, landing gear are a plane's wheels and the flaps are an extension towards the back end of the wings. When the flaps are extended/down, it increases the amount of lift that the wings generate, whilst also allowing the plane to fly slower and thus land (and reverse for take-off).

In that same vein, let me close this out with some final thoughts;

I am not sure I learned much, except to have deep empathy and understanding for others.

Despite my efforts, I survived the year, which may or may not be a good thing – this is a TBD. It certainly has been a year though.

So whereto next after I land this plane? What does tomorrow look like for Nico? October? 2024?

Simply, I do not know. As I eluded to in earlier chapters, I learned to not trust mental health professionals, so I will definitely be a lot more guarded in future. But I am also an incredibly naive person – much more naive than most people you're bound to meet, and I struggle to imagine that someone would try deceive me on purpose. I might yet end up in that hospital again, I am fairly sure of that.

However, *right now, right this moment – at 17:09 on 28 September 2023*, I am OK. Much more OK than I have been in a while. And that is saying something. It's like Psalm 23 says "though I walk through the valley of the shadow of Death...", I certainly think I have walked out of the valley. I no longer feel and sense Death's cold breath in the corner of the room. So maybe that in itself is an improvement?

As I emerge from the Valley of Death, my eyes need some time to adjust to the Light and Life. So I might need some time. I think that is one thing I have learned; Getting better – especially mentally – is not a given, nor a linear/exponential thing. Improving mental health is like the tides of the ocean that ebb and flow. Perhaps in future, I will be more kind and merciful with myself than I have been. Maybe that was the big lesson I had to learn.

I've maintained contact with a few patients that I met when I was in the hospital. One thing that has surprised me in every conversation, was how much they missed "my table" – as in the table with the ugly mustard yellow chair I used to sit at, available for anyone to talk with or at.

It didn't seem like such a big deal *at the time*. From my own experience, it seemed as if there might be others who were not only equally lonely (though I rarely feel the need to socialise), but more importantly to talk about how they feel, why they feel – without judgement.

I didn't think anyone would really remember it. But I have had some very surprising, heart-warming comments about the fact that I made myself available and vulnerable.

Alarmingly though, it seems the need for that sort of function still exists. For someone to sit in an ugly mustard yellow chair, open to people walking up to at random, and being open to talking about whatever, even if it includes – no – especially if it means talking about things like mental health issues.

To listen and not judge. To listen and not advise. To listen and not lock up. But most importantly, to have been through that deep, dark valley of Death and stand at the other side with arms waiting wide open, encouraging others to put one foot in front of the next. One step after the other, no matter how long it takes. To wait there for them and cheer them on to victory.

I just wish someone like that existed who isn't me. You know? Despite being in a much better place mentally than I was on page 1, I have very little faith in myself. I've learned by now that most ideas I have are mud.

So my idea to be a facilitator to a group – like AA in a way – where people (men?) can come to and openly share and talk about their struggles with mental health and suicidal thoughts is a BAD idea. I should DEFINITELY NOT do that.

If only there were such a person though. It seems that beyond psychologists and all other manner of -ists, there is need for someone to say "Hey man, I've been through that dark valley and I made it out. Here, I will walk that with you".

Maybe in the future a great man will arise to be that light to others in the darkness. It's certainly not a job for a dick on a donkey...

So that's it.

Rest assured that I am measurably better than I was on page 1.

I have a semblance of Hope for the future, small as it might be. I am preparing for job interviews, I am planning a YouTube channel to discuss nerdy Mathematics in movies and generally feeling more optimistic.

My parting words would be;

If someone you know is walking through the Valley of Death;
Just love them. Honestly, and sincerely, just love them. Go to bed with a humble, grateful heart that it is not *you* in that position, for you might well have broken long ago. Do not judge those who are going through such a deep pit of despair. Humans do not *choose* to feel so hopeless, that ending their lives seem like a viable way out. Love, support, encourage and just be there. Be like my friend who listened to, and laughed about my experience, laughed raucously about my ridiculous notion for surprise euthanasia and who has continued to be a friend for me ever since. You do not know it, and your person might not be able to articulate it; But your presence and non-judgmental support means more than you can ever imagine.

If you are walking through the Valley of Death;

My Friend, you do not walk alone. If you do not find a great man to walk with, and you're happy for a Dick on a Donkey to accompany you, I will walk it with you. Know that yes, the Valley might be long and full of thorns. But take one step after the other and you will get through it. Getting better isn't instant or quick. But you can get better. Just give yourself the kindness and space to feel what you feel. Then take one more step. Your story is not over until it is over. YOU might be the great man we all need to facilitate those meetings I spoke of. So walk through that Valley and stand in the breech for others. And even if you cannot stand in the breech for others, maybe the only one you need to stand up for is yourself.

Either way, I wish you peace.

And to you dear reader, if you have read this far, please go buy yourself a medal. You deserve it for reading this utter mess and chaos of random thoughts!

POTENTIAL NEW RESEARCH FOR
MENTAL HEALTH (Mental Health people, please read)

Preface: This might not be universally true for all Neurodivergent people, but it might be a smoking gun we have not considered before. But I think it is true for me;

I am pretty handy with DIY and tools.

My hammer especially.

It's a pretty neat hammer - I use it to hammer in nails, wood screws, rivets - even rawl bolts. I've also fixed my wife's porcelain teapot with it, as well as a crystal ornament of mine. It did not seem to work so well on the teapot or ornament. Instead of fixing them, the hammer seems to have turned the porcelain and teapots into smaller bits. But I am convinced that my approach is sound - I am very careful when I fix fragile things with the hammer. It's the only tool I have really, but seems to work well enough.

It occurred to me that Mental Health professionals also have hammers. Small ones, rubber ones, massive big ones - a great variety of hammers. For the most part, their hammers work...

OK, I'll leave the hammer analogy there. You get the picture. If all you have is a hammer, everything looks like a nail.

BUT HOLY COW! A REALISATION STRUCK ME YESTERDAY LIKE A WET FISH IN THE FACE!

I could not see anything much online that speaks to what I am saying below, but I think I might have inadvertently stumbled upon a possible reason for the disproportionately high suicide rates among Neurodivergent people.

Of those with ASD (Autism), 66% have at some point thought about suicide and an incredible 35% have attempted suicide! Some studies show that Autistic adults are 9x more likely to die by suicide than the general population. It's a fairly similar story for people with ADHD - higher suicide risks and rates than the general population.

BUT I DO NOT THINK IT IS DEPRESSION!

Autism and ADHD have a bit of an overlap in one area in terms of hobbies & interests; Obsession and hyperfixation. They're different - I'll briefly outline;

AUTISTIC OBSESSION:
The cliched image with Autistic Obsession is boys/men being obsessed with Trains. There are other examples like having an obsession with Star Trek, LEGO, Dinosaurs, Computer Coding etc. But the point is that Autistic individuals have this life-long obsession with a handful of topics. But they pursue them passionately and intensely. Whatever it is, you cannot easily change an Autistic Obsession...

ADHD HYPERFIXATION:
ADHD hyperfixation is generally similar to Autistic Obsession. But the difference is that with ADHD, these hyperfixations are often significantly shorter in duration; Weeks, Months - maybe years. But generally quite short lived. This is why there is this cliched example of people with ADHD who have a hundred different hobbies/interests scattered all around the house. As with the Autistic counterparts, people with ADHD pursue their hyperfixation very intensely. Perhaps even more so than their counterparts. To the point that they lose sense of time or environment. Whatever it is, you cannot easily change an ADHD Hyperfixation...

SO WHAT?
Well... So what indeed. I'm sure you can see where I am going with this. Autistic and ADHD people (AuDHD for Autism & ADHD for people with both) often have additional issues with mental health. Because we lack the ability to make sense of all of the issues we have in life, we don't have the coping mechanisms that normal

people have. We often have "meltdowns" which is a profound impairment in our ability to think and operate rationally.

When our lives suddenly crash; Lose a job/home - whatever major negative life change (perceived or real) we suddenly are even more unable to cope! During a mental crisis, we cannot think clearly about how to handle the crisis, so our thoughts turn to a "fix". But we are also utterly and completely overwhelmed by crises - we have "meltdowns". Instead of just being a "naughty little shit" thing, meltdowns are absolutely horrific. Our executive functioning stops. Shuts down. The only other alternative we can then come up with, is to end the problem. Us being the problem. Death being the end.

It's not - and I have to stress this - IT IS NOT THAT WE NECESSARILY WANT TO DIE. We want the pain to end. We want the trouble to end. But because of our executive dysfunction, we cannot think of any other way out.

SO DEATH BECOMES THE MACABRE OBSESSION / HYPERFIXATION! Like a macabre hobby. But instead of the hobby being something innocent like Trains, Dinosaurs of LEGO, it's something much more insidious.

The "fix" for our lives becomes a obsession /hyperfixation, and that is the only fix we can see. Because our executive functioning becomes so impaired, we cannot think of a different solution. We're like deer in headlights.

For Autistic people, it is their obsession - not like in "study out of interest" - it becomes the obsession with how to fix their problem. For ADHD, it becomes the fix - the literal hyperfixation on how to fix their problem. And it is a hyperfixation that will not rest until it is achieved.

Think of anyone with ADHD how when they decide they want a new camera/LEGO set/ Computer - whatever - they literally do not rest until they've "scratched that itch".

HOLY COW, DO YOU REALISE THE IMPLICATION HERE??

Mental Health professionals have clearly not (at least in my case) studied this. Or realised this. At least not from this perspective. I've not once seen or heard it being discussed. Hell, it takes months (years?) on the NHS to just get diagnosed with ADHD or Autism!! So mental health professionals do not seem to consider this in their treatment.

I mean all they do is use the hammers in their toolkit;
Depression.
Antidepressants.
"Oh, you want to kill yourself? Must be depression".

So they diagnose us with depression, causing further embarrassment and stigma in us. They put us on antidepressants which are quite capable of making things worse. Many antidepressants actually cause Autistic and ADHD people to then go on to commit suicide. It pushes us over the edge.

They put people like me in mental hospitals. I have from the start maintained I do not have depression. And this sudden realisation confirms this. I had an Autistic Obsession - an ADHD HYPERFIXATION about ending my life, because my executive functioning had shut down completely.

Frak me.

I also as I am typing this, realised that my suicidal thoughts only truly ended when I discovered I had ADHD and guess what? I became hyper-fixated on learning about ADHD and its effects. My hyperfixation jumped from committing suicide to studying ADHD. Then of course I started studying, got a student loan with a grant (which helped pay bills a bit) and an absolutely exquisite job which all took my hyperfixation off of suicide.

Most people are never assessed for Autism or ADHD. Most are only now in late adulthood officially diagnosed. So those with these conditions do not understand themselves and mental health professionals either do not understand, or do not see the connection between Hyperfixation or Obsession on suicide as one might on Dinosaurs or LEGO.

Mental Health Professionals; SOMEONE STUDY THIS PLEASE.

We could treat people with Autism, ADHD and other Neurodivergent conditions so much better if we just stop using fucking hammers to fix porcelain teapots.

THE CHEQUERED FLAG – FINALLY 20 May 2024

Today, a year ago, my wife, a friend and I sat on the grass outside a mental hospital in mid-Wales, eating cheese Domino's pizza.

So much has happened since I last wrote in mid-October 2023;

My beloved 14 year old cat had to be put down because he had heart failure. A traumatising 2 week period where we tried to give him medicine and help him, to the vet finally needing to come to my house. My poor cat spent that Monday afternoon struggling for breath and in crisis, until the vet arrived and injected him. I felt his last heartbeat. Felt when the life left him. It broke me. It broke me broken. I did actually try to commit suicide after that, I was just too broken. It caused a lot of trouble for me as I was evidently resuscitated, and had to apologise to people I hurt.

But I have been going for counselling regularly and things are improving overall. In some areas slower than others, but overall improving.

I started studying a degree, which only lasted about 2 months, as I got really busy at work!

Work? Yes. Work. I finally found a job. Rather, the job found me. I am now an IT & Data lecturer. I teach people Data Literacy and how to use various software tools etc. It's a job that has brought me a profound sense of fulfilment. A year ago, I wrote about wanting to help people and this is honestly helping me do that in a practical way.

In jest, I often bet people £1.39 that they will learn something new. Particularly in the Microsoft Excel Advanced classes. I've taught many people and to date, my £1.39 is safe! It's been so enjoyable to help people – but also to earn an income.

The job started off as a very part-time thing. But because I had extra time, and did well in it, there was opportunity to get more involved. But it did mean my time was being soaked up and I did not have time for my University studies. I got 75% and 74% for my first two major assignments, which was great. But I needed to free up some time as I was not able to cope with so much.

Which I guess is a healthy thing – being mindful of my limitations and requesting a pause on my studies.

But perhaps the greatest help for me in the last 6 or so months, was learning that I have ADHD. Whilst I am still waiting for an official diagnosis, 3 separate psychiatrists have so far said that I have ADHD.

I've also learned a great deal about ADHD – it is not just the "Hyperactive Naughty Boy" thing that society seems to think it is. In fact, ADHD is a profoundly serious condition that has very, very serious ramifications in a person's life.

It's not just about having poor discipline and just needing a proper hiding either. There is a difference in the way people's brains are physically made up. Take for example the fact that all my life, I could not understand the societal "joke" that coffee helps keep you awake. Because caffeine makes me sleepy. I did not realise this, until per chance, I was reading about ADHD medication and stimulants.

I thought it weird that people with ADHD would be given *stimulants*... But in my case, it seems that the caffeine in Monster and Red Bull energy drinks has a paradoxical effect which makes me very chill and relaxed. So much so, that I started experimenting with taking 200mg caffeine tablets. It's the weirdest thing, but about 30 – 45 minutes before going to bed, I take a 200mg caffeine tablet and I cannot keep my eyes open. I tested it very scientifically of course, taking it at different times, different days, weekends etc. But there is a very clear correlation for me.

There's a lot more ways in which ADHD impacts a person – some of which I have written about already.

The point is; For the first time in my entire life, I am at peace.

Truly at peace.

Finally putting the pieces of my fractured being together by realising I am Autistic with ADHD has allowed me to fully understand myself and why I react and behave in ways I do. Think of it like the "Theory of Everything" – a theory, set of Mathematical principles if you will – that describes the large cosmological scale of the universe, down to the quantum level.

Basically, the ability to fully understand the Universe and everything in it.

Learning about Autism and ADHD and how I am driven and affected by it has been probably the single-most driver in my recovery from 2023. Throughout the pages of this… "writing", I struggled with various things, struggled to understand. It goes beyond just what I wrote here, my entire life has been a desperate attempt to understand the world and why I react in the ways I do. Why I think like I do.

But now that I know better about Autism and ADHD (and perhaps other conditions I choose to not share), I am able to understand myself better. By understanding myself better, I've been able to accept and love myself better.

And though there is arguably a great journey ahead in terms of truly getting to know and love myself fully, at least I've started on the journey. A stark contrast to a year ago!

I am not suggesting that diagnosing everyone with a neurological condition like Autism or ADHD is the way to fix people's mental health. In some ways it might damage them more.

But for me, it would have been enormously more helpful if medical professionals – Mental Health Professionals especially – tried to understand the way my brain works instead of telling me I have depression and shoving me full of pills.

From the start of this book, I have insisted that I do not have a mental health illness. I have issues with chronic back pain that still give me sleepless nights and cause me pain. Though the 50+ kg in weight I lost between October 2022 and January 2024 has helped take a lot of strain off my spine, and I think definitely improved things a bit.

I'm still not super optimistic about the future. There are days when I try think ahead about what the future may bring, but then I feel like the story of when Jesus walked on water and Peter tried to join him. But when Peter saw the waves and the wind, he got afraid and started sinking.

That's how I feel when I look to the future – like the tumult of uncertainty is dragging me in.

But as long as I don't do that, I am fine.

I recall in the mental hospital, I used to think to myself "*Just listen to this song. Just try survive until the end of this song*". That's how I made it through that time when things got too much – I'd tell myself to not try think ahead too far, but just survive for the next 30 seconds. Or minute – or until the end of a song. Once the song finished and the uncertainty returned, I'd put the same (or different) song on, and try survive just for that next song.

I no longer listen to music as a survival tool all the time. I now listen to it for the enjoyment of the music again. From time to time, yes, I just try survive a song. But I am able to walk on my own on the water a bit. Though I still get filled with panic when I look ahead at the chasm of uncertainty.

But in all, I think from where I was 1 year ago, I am a very different person. There are things I wrote in these pages that I should never have written. That nobody should ever write. But it's a reflection of where I was mentally, which was not a good place.

I've struggled with feeling worthless to feeling useful and like I make a measurable difference in people's lives.
I've been frustrated at myself for not understand Life and people, to learning that I am just assembled differently and having more grace and acceptance towards myself for my differences.
I've gone from spending every waking moment, trying to think of how to end my life, to thinking of how I can make other people's lives better and easier.

So that's where I will leave this. A glimpse into probably the worst year of my life, descending into chaos and coming out with a kinder, more caring world view, greater self-acceptance – and shockingly perhaps even a dash of love for myself.

Printed in Great Britain
by Amazon

43490915R10145